# REINVENTING SOCIAL SECURITY WORLDWIDE

## Back to essentials

Vladimir Rys

This edition published in Great Britain in 2010 by

The Policy Press
University of Bristol
Fourth Floor
Beacon House
Queen's Road
Bristol BS8 1QU
UK

t: +44 (0)117 331 4054
f: +44 (0)117 331 4093
e: tpp-info@bristol.ac.uk
www.policypress.co.uk

North American office:
The Policy Press
c/o International Specialized Books Services
920 NE 58th Avenue, Suite 300
Portland, OR 97213-3786, USA
t: +1 503 287 3093
f: +1 503 280 8832
e: info@isbs.com

British Library Cataloguing in Publication Data
A catalogue record for this book is available from the British Library.

Library of Congress Cataloging-in-Publication Data
A catalog record for this book has been requested.

ISBN 978 1 84742 640 6  paperback
ISBN 978 1 84742 641 3  hardcover

Cover design by Qube Design Associates, Bristol
Front cover: image kindly supplied by iStock
Printed and bound in Great Britain by Hobbs, Southampton

# Contents

# About the author

Born in 1928 in what was then Czechoslovakia, Vladimir Rys interrupted his studies at Charles University in Prague after the communist coup d'état in 1948 and came to England. After a period of manual work he was awarded a grant to study sociology at the London School of Economics and Political Science (LSE) and subsequently went to the Sorbonne to write a doctoral thesis comparing social security in France and in Great Britain. On returning to the LSE in 1958 he worked as senior research assistant to professor R.M. Titmuss.

In 1960 he joined the staff of the International Social Security Association (ISSA) in Geneva and was responsible for the organisation of research and documentation activities of this worldwide body of social security administrations. In 1975 he was appointed ISSA secretary general.

On retirement in 1990 he returned to academic research devoted mainly to the sociological study of social security reforms in Central Europe. This activity included short-term teaching assignments at Charles University, co-direction of a study centre at the University of Geneva and presentation of papers to different professional organisations. His study on social security reform in the Czech Republic (*La sécurité sociale dans une société en transition: l'expérience tchèque* [*Social Security in a Society in Transition: The Czech Experience*]) was published in 1999 in Switzerland.

With the present book the author returns to his former preoccupations concerning social security developments worldwide and reacts to the challenge that is now facing the institution.

# Foreword

In the late 1960s, as a doctoral student at Cornell University, I read Vladimir Rys's pioneering seminal essay published in 1964 on the application of macro-sociological factor analysis to social security and it significantly influenced my future research and career. Under the auspices of the Social Science Research Council, in the summer of 1976, I took 20 doctoral students, half from the US and half from Latin America, to an Inter-American training seminar held in Mexico City on the application of social sciences techniques to social security. Rys's analysis of internal and external variables influencing the inception and evolution of social security, which at the time had generated an international debate, was a central topic of stimulating discussions in the said seminar. My first book on social security published in the US was inspired by Rys. Relying on his analysis of pressure groups and the role of the state in social security inception, I developed a taxonomy for Latin America to show how multiple social insurance funds segmented along occupational lines had induced stratification, and used Rys's factor analysis to measure the resulting social security inequality in the region (Mesa-Lago, 1978). And now we are members of the Editorial Consultant Board of the *International Social Security Review*. Four decades after our first virtual encounter, he continues to be a master in the field and it is an honour to write this foreword to his book *Reinventing Social Security Worldwide: Back to Essentials*.

The book is an excellent, sophisticated and well-integrated compendium of many important topics in the field, a useful review of the literature, an update of the author's previous contribution on the application of macro-sociological factor analysis to social security, and a proposal for reinventing social security in order to save it. Rys's main thesis and goal is to 'preserve social insurance as the basic social security technique, conceived in its original form as a contract between the individual and society' (p 2), by reinforcing this tool of social protection, adapting it to current needs and financial-political possibilities, and using it to confront the adverse social effects of the current global economic crisis.

This is a very timely book as the grave crisis is affecting social protection in developed and developing countries and there is already an ongoing effort by international organisations to find solutions. Furthermore, the crisis has made evident the policy error made in the last three decades by the neoliberal ideology imposed on many nations, sharply reducing the role of the state and enlarging that of the market and the private sector, without appropriate regulation and supervision.

According to Rys, 'The neoliberal ideology ... gave rise to a false confidence in the superiority of private individual arrangements for guaranteeing income security over collective provisions' (p 6). In 1994, the World Bank proposed a new pension paradigm: a system of 'pillars' including a mandatory defined contribution, fully funded pillar based on individual accounts and managed by private for-profit firms to replace the conventional defined benefit, pay-as-you-go (or partial collective capitalisation), publicly managed schemes (World Bank, 1994). As Rys notes, the industrialised countries did not follow said paradigm but several developing and emerging countries did. Under the Pinochet government, Chile implemented a pioneering structural pension reform in 1981, followed in the 1990s and the first decade of the 21st century by nine other countries in Latin America and many new democracies in Eastern Europe, which totally or partially privatised their public pension programmes. The shortcomings of the new private systems (disregard of poverty prevention, accentuation of gender discrimination, lack of social solidarity and social participation), and the fact that the praxis showed opposite results to their presumed beneficial effects (decline in coverage, inadequate competition, high administrative costs, poor compliance, improper portfolio diversification), were ignored by international financial organisations and policy makers for two decades despite criticism from some scholars, including myself. In 2005, the World Bank published a book reassessing its policies in Latin America in the previous decade, which acknowledged some of the cited flaws (Gill et al, 2005).

Since 2007-08, a reversal trend has been taking place in that region where two countries have counter-reformed their privatised pension programmes, leading to divergent approaches: Chile's comprehensive reform has improved the system, infusing it with universality, social solidarity and equity, whereas Argentina has shut down its private scheme and integrated it with the remaining public one. Other countries have followed or are considering one of the two approaches (Mesa-Lago, 2009). The current crisis is contributing to this re-reform process that hopefully will lead to a return of the key principles of social insurance although adapted to current realities. Rys pinpoints such reversal, and advocates it and the need to reinvigorate social insurance 'tested by more than 100 years of experience' (p 6).

Another main topic of the book is the significant reduction in the role of the state in social security, transferring its responsibility to individual savings, family support, employer and occupational schemes, private insurance and social assistance, which have resulted in diminished social protection, increased inequality, weakening of social insurance and its replacement by social aid. The general trend towards the retrenchment of the welfare state has led to deterioration in its main programmes of pensions and healthcare. Rys calls for a turnaround of such a trend by strengthening and introducing changes in mandatory social security in order to guarantee minimum benefits to individuals against major social risks. Rys argues, however, that the initial goals of social insurance are no longer financially feasible, due to lower economic growth in industrialised economies, population ageing and maturity of pension schemes that increases costs to intolerable levels. Hence the need to 'reinvent' social insurance to guarantee minimum benefits to all the population, reduce its redistributive function, assure its transparency so that each person can assess the cost-benefit of their participation, rely on the principle of a social right, and leave to individuals and the private sector (under state regulation) the provision of supplementary benefits to maintain the desired level of living. He also establishes a difference in policy between developed countries (which should maintain social insurance) and developing countries (where social insurance has stagnated and been partly replaced by tax-financed basic programmes for large masses of rural and informal workers). He warns against the risk involved in implementing a global social security floor for all and tax-financed benefits.

The book is structured into three parts. Part One deals with the world evolution of social security. In Chapter One, Rys recounts the predecessors of social insurance, the latter evolution to social security, its zenith of world influence, and its retrenchment since the mid-1970s; this is the best summary I have read on the subject and includes new insights. Chapter Two deals with some essential issues of social protection: (1) argues that income redistribution is essentially an instrument of fiscal and not social policy, clarifies a common confusion between the social insurance and income-redistribution functions, and defends the need to separate both and return to the original goal of social insurance – to protect individuals against social risks – and leave to the taxation system the income-redistribution role; (2) stresses the need to fully integrate social security and economic policy as exemplified by the European Union; (3) conducts fascinating historical analyses of social security under diverse socio-politico-economic systems: communism (arguing that the debate on communist social 'inventions' is not dead), neoliberalism (contrasting the World Bank and the International Labour Organization approaches to social security), and democracy (in theory, social security fulfils its mission only in a democratic society but Rys questions whether that institution is properly used in practice). In Chapter Three, Rys contends that neoliberal approaches have lost momentum and social security is regaining respectability, hence there is a window of opportunity to reform it. He proposes to adapt social security to new societal conditions, but cautions against certain new trends and advocates a drastic reform with different approaches for developed and developing countries – he argues that to ensure the long-term development of social insurance it must be politically acceptable, economically affordable and transparent.

Part Two examines the methodology to understand social security in its societal milieu. Chapter Four is an interesting history of the evolution of the sociology of social security (various stages between the early 1960s and 2000) as well as the application of other social science approaches to social security. In Chapter Five, Rys applies macro-sociological factor analysis to social security, based on internal and external factors important in the inception and development of social security: internal factors belong to the internal environment of a society, such as demographic, economic, sociological and political, whereas external factors are international cultural transfers like ideas, laws and techniques of social protection, diffusion means, and the role of international organisations. Chapter Six examines the use of macro-sociological factor analysis in comparative studies in post-communist societies in the early years of the 21st century.

Part Three explains the ways to adapt social security to the new societal environment, particularly in the midst of the global economic crisis, and in pursuit of long-term financial sustainability. Rys proposes the creation of adequate reserves for the periods of crisis, provided directly from the economy and set independently from customary social security financing; he also asks for transparency of operations with information provided to each insured person in order to assess the cost and benefits of their participation, and thus recover the lost confidence on social insurance.

One important point that should stir debate is Rys's quest for a complete separation of social insurance and social assistance and the preservation of the former as the basic social technique and conceived in its original form. In some of my works I have asked for administrative and financial separation of both instruments of social security in order to protect social insurance funds and force the state to take financial responsibility for social assistance. I do agree also that Rys's pursuit is feasible in developed countries with a labour force essentially urban and formal. But I have doubts that such a goal is feasible in poor developing countries where most of the labour force is informal and rural, and therefore excluded from social insurance or, at best, offered legal voluntary affiliation that is ineffective. In half of the countries in Latin America, social insurance covers a minority of the labour force and the population, usually in the middle-income strata, and often receives fiscal subsidies that are regressive as they come from consumer taxes paid by all the population including the excluded. This is also true in many poor countries in Africa and Asia. The possibility of rapidly expanding social insurance coverage in such nations is remote; for instance, the Latin American trend in the last 30 years showed increasing informality, except for the period 2004-07 due to the economic boom, now reversed by the world crisis. One could also argue that the employer's contribution in some cases is transferred to consumers, hence accentuating the regressive impact of the system. Facing scarce resources, these countries should give priority to basic benefits for their poor and low-income people, starting with primary healthcare, nutrition and education. Rys is right that the state should be charged with the fundamental redistributing function, but the minority covered by social insurance in those countries should not receive fiscal subsidies that must be targeted on vulnerable groups. The International Social Security Association (ISSA) established in 2008 a Task Group for Extension of Coverage that I chair and is working on these controversial issues; we intend to elaborate guidelines for ISSA members that take into account significant socioeconomic differences among countries.

This book will have a long shelf life as it deals with historical issues and analytical tools that have resisted the passage of time. It will be useful for policy makers, staff of international and regional financial and social organisations and social security associations, as well as research scholars, teachers, graduate and undergraduate students, and social security professionals and administrators. It should serve as an excellent textbook on social welfare courses or a supplementary text in courses in economics, sociology, political science and history related to social policy, development and similar themes. It is my hope that Rys continues inspiring future generations of social security scholars and experts.

*Carmelo Mesa-Lago, Distinguished Service Professor Emeritus of Economics, University of Pittsburgh and Chair of the ISSA task force on the extension of social security coverage*

# Introduction

The world economy is going through a serious crisis, which is having an impact on all types of societal institutions. Social security is in the front line, both on account of the volume of its financial flows and on account of its importance for the preservation of the minimum standard of living of every individual. This seems to be an opportune moment to review briefly the way the institution has developed since its beginnings, take note of the changes that have taken place in its societal environment and in the perception of its overall mission and bring home a few lessons to serve as guidelines for a necessary reorientation of its path.

The global trends in the evolution of the institution prior to the onset of the world financial crisis were already indicating the presence of some negative features representing risks for the continuation of its mission. In industrial societies, no new social protection mechanism has been invented to deal with new risks and socially precarious situations. What has happened has been a series of shifts in emphasis on different elements in the existing social security structures and in the roles assigned to specific actors. Thus, the state, while reducing its direct involvement in the actual running of social security schemes, has been greatly increasing its powers regarding the regulation of occupational and private arrangements. And there has been a shift of responsibility back to employers and different forms of occupational welfare, back to families and their supporting role and also back to individual citizens and their personal capacity to save. While some of these features may be considered as a step towards a more appropriate equilibration of respective responsibilities, the move towards the disengagement of the state is an obvious historical regression; it has gone too far and – as shown by the present evidence of the state's decisive role in economic governance – its equivalent role in social matters needs to be reaffirmed.

Another important global trend points towards an increasing mix in the sources of finance of social welfare measures and in the benefits they provide often in a way unrelated to their principal mission. Thus, social insurance financing may have a frequent resort to ad hoc taxation while social insurance benefits may often be used for purposes suggesting an ongoing 'instrumentalisation' of social security for the achievement of other goals of public policy, be it with regard to employment or with regard to measures used to combat social exclusion.[1] This development calls for extreme caution, since – reflecting a very short-term and purely economic approach to welfare measures – it could eventually lead to the replacement of social insurance with social aid. In the past, these two institutions have always followed a different logic both with regard to sources of finance and with regard to the destination and scope of benefits and any attempt at blurring the frontiers between them for reason of financial expediency is bound to be detrimental to the long-term objective of preventing destitution in the midst of our societies.

This same trend can also be detected in the developing world, although starting from a completely different premise. The economic decline of the final decades of the 20th century has put an end to the rapid expansion of social security and led even to its regression in some regions of the world. Since economic perspectives are now less favourable than in the past, there has been a change in public expectations with regard to social protection measures. Worldwide programmes for the fight against poverty, launched by leading international organisations, have given impetus to a claim that, without waiting for a gradual extension of social security coverage some measures be taken instantly in favour of the vast masses of the rural population. The outcome is a plan for the creation of tax-financed programmes for what is described as basic social security.

Such an abrupt change in the orientation of social security policy requires of course an extremely careful consideration. If the intention is to proceed to some kind of nation-wide redistribution of available income, that income has to be first created before it can be redistributed, which also means that this plan can hardly be carried out without competing for scarce resources with the existing social security establishment. Moreover, as people working in the field already point out, the logic of tax-financed social security directly undermines the concept of social insurance based on the idea of self-help through the financial contribution of the insured population. The problem hence consists of how to achieve coordination in the build-up of these two very distinct types of social protection measures, bearing in mind the long-term objective.

In this book we defend the thesis for which the present world economic crisis has provided new supporting evidence. Given the prevailing economic order, it is imperative to preserve social insurance as the basic social security technique, conceived in its original form as a contract between the individual and society, so as to make it possible to effectively guarantee an individual's minimum living conditions. The state must continue to provide the basic institutional framework for obligatory social insurance requiring the financial participation of all citizens in a scheme, which can protect them against the consequences of the materialisation of major social risks. It would be irresponsible, in the light of recent experience, to entrust this task to private arrangements.

Only supplementary benefits ensuring the maintenance of a desired standard of living should be left to individual effort.

In view of the political evolution and present attitudes of the general public towards social security, it would seem reasonable to undertake steps so as to gradually reduce the volume of income redistribution generated by these schemes since the post-war years prior to the first oil shock, when the intention was to maintain the standard of living previously achieved by the individual. This objective being no longer economically attainable through public social protection provisions, the goal should be to guarantee a minimum standard of living, politically acceptable to all classes of the population and affordable within the volume of the resources provided by the economy. At the same time, the income flows engendered by the revised social insurance schemes should be made transparent so as to enable every insured person to evaluate the cost and benefits of their participation. Only such policy of full transparency can prevent further deterioration of the status of the institution in the eyes of the majority of the population and a further move towards an unbalanced growth of private arrangements for the well-off classes accompanied by growing reliance on social assistance provisions for the less fortunate.

The arguments to support the above thesis are developed in three parts of the book. Part One deals with the institution of social security in a global perspective. First, it reviews the main stages of its development until the present time. In the light of recent experience, we conclude that the vision of a progressive adaptation of social security institutions to the gradual reduction of economic growth, plausible in the closing years of the preceding millennium, has now been deeply shattered by two successive disruptions of international financial and economic functions. If the existing capitalist market machinery finds its way back to another spell of continuing growth, the chances are that those successful individuals who regain prosperity will fully embrace the neoliberal credo and its preference for social assistance measures for the weak. But if the comeback is slow and socially painful, it is likely to provoke revolutionary movements and attempts to overthrow the existing social and economic order. Whatever the case may be, it seems evident that a major reappraisal of existing trends in social security policy is needed to bring the institution into the front line of defence of a socially just and democratic society.

Chapter Two is devoted to the discussion of a number of essential issues of contemporary social security policy on which we take a stand that does not necessarily comply with mainstream attitudes. They include the problem of full integration of social and economic policies, which requires a fundamental rethinking of some current practices and calls for an unreserved acceptance of the original mission of social security, before the institution is lost among accessories of economic policies. Worldwide ideological links to social security are subsequently examined, first in relation to the experience under communism, then in the light of the criticism formulated by the neoliberal school of thought.

This chapter also deals with two societal values, solidarity and democracy, which are indispensable to the true concept of social security. The type of solidarity expressed in the concept of social insurance puts a special emphasis on the notions of self-help, personal independence and equality of citizens when faced with adversity. The institution permits the individual to adopt what some may consider as an old-fashioned attitude of refusal of charity or, to use a more recent terminology, a third-party discretionary aid, and to give preference to benefit as of right guaranteed by the social security scheme. This characteristic is of particular value for the maintenance of the civic spirit of independence, which is of crucial importance for social development. With regard to democracy, we emphasise that social security is not only an income maintenance technique for certain contingencies, that is, a defensive measure ensuring protection against socials risks, but also, and above all, an offensive measure ensuring freedom of full participation in social life. The recognition of this fact leads to the obligation to make value judgements when estimating the quality of the institution within its societal environment.

Chapter Three analyses in more detail the progressive decline in the performance of social security schemes over the last two decades and examines emerging trends in the evolution of the institution. This overview, which concerns both the industrialised and developing countries, indicates the presence of questionable non-systemic approaches in searching for solutions to current difficulties.

Part Two intends to get the reader acquainted with a convenient tool for a better understanding of social security. It is devoted to a macro-sociological analysis of the institution permitting a global approach to its evolution while identifying the chief factors shaping its development. It presents, first, an overview of the early history of the sociological study of social security from its beginnings in the 1960s to the close of the 20th century. Subsequently it deals with a revised and updated version of what has come to be viewed as a seminal work on the sociology of social security, penned by the author within the framework of the research programme of the International Social Security Association (ISSA) in Geneva and originally published in 1964. The message of this earlier study is still valid today: the development of social security – and the welfare state more generally – must be understood in the broad interconnected context of economic, social and political factors present in the institution's societal environment; in this sense, it seems to be directly linked to the current mainstream research.[2] The last chapter of Part Two is devoted to the use of macro-sociological factor analysis in more recent comparative studies.

In Part Three, an attempt is made to outline foundations for a new political consensus on social security corresponding to the urgent need for an adaptation of the institution to the new societal environment and particularly to the requirement of long-term economic sustainability. To the extent that the maintenance of the social security institution appears to be essential for the preservation of the existing world order, its economic sustainability should be ensured by constituting adequate financial reserves for the periods of economic crises and dysfunctions of the economic system. These funds should be entirely independent from regular social security financing and should be provided directly by the economy, possibly through levies on excessive salaries of leaders of financial institutions or any other type of excessive remuneration of an economic activity. Such a measure could also cover levies on proceeds of speculative investments that, as much as excessive salaries, contribute to the creation of periodic crises in the economic system.

To ensure a wide political consensus, the requirement of economic sustainability has to be accompanied by the requirement of transparency of social security operations. In order to regain the lost confidence of the public, the social security schemes of the future will have to be perfectly transparent in their operations, indicating to every insured person the cost of their total contribution effort and the benefit obtained. If accompanied by appropriate information effort, this transparency should not result in any rejection of solidarity inherent in the concept of social insurance by the upper-income classes. In view of the magnitude of the costs involved in ensuring the security of individual existence through private means, this solidarity effort may go a long way supported by a sense of self-interest.

The somewhat unusual approach to the study of social security presented in this book has been dictated by the author's life experience. In real life, the institution writes its own history and social science runs after it, trying to explain it the best it can. The essential thing is to understand the institutional evolution in its historical context so as to provide a meaningful answer to the question 'why are things what they are?' For this exercise, a sharp sense of observation and an open mind are more important than a multitude of analytical concepts. Understanding the sense of evolution of a social institution helps to determine what kind of social policy, in given societal conditions, is suitable for achieving its objectives.

Recent decades have given us an opportunity to make a number of fundamental observations. In the example of the communist countries we have been able to watch the futility of the totalitarian collectivist approach to guaranteeing people an acceptable standard of living. In their relatively short-lived experiment, the economic system was unable to bear the cost. But even if that burden had been made supportable, the vast majority of the population would still refuse to pay the price; in the last analysis, political freedom was considered more valuable and more apt to guarantee personal and material security of everyday life than social benefits of the communist society.

The neoliberal ideology credo that in many countries replaced the communist doctrine practically overnight and without any critical judgement gave rise to a false confidence in the superiority of private individual arrangements for guaranteeing income security over collective provisions. However, financial markets follow different objectives and have different priorities than social protection institutions. Following an international financial crash early in the new millennium, the present deep crisis of the whole economic system has provided a definite proof of the fallacy of the social doctrine of neoliberal ideology and of the need for a new approach to the concept of social security. Admittedly, our proposal to return back to the grassroots of the institution does not convey a great impression of novelty, but it has at least the merit of stepping on a firm ground tested by more than 100 years of experience.

## Notes

[1] This trend is explained in more detail in Chapter Three.

[2] 'Recent approaches to state welfare have in common that they are sensitive to the interaction of economic, social and political factors in welfare state stability and change, and are aware that all these dimensions must be taken into account' (Taylor-Gooby, 2002, p 602).

# Part One

# Social security evolution in a global perspective: what is at stake?

# ONE

# A brief history of social security

There is no generally accepted and generally applicable definition of social security. What is most frequently referred to is the whole set of compulsory measures adopted by society to protect the individual and their family against the consequences of an unavoidable interruption or serious diminution of the earned income needed for maintaining a reasonable standard of living. This has the advantage of reducing the field of investigation to more concrete institutional or institutionalised measures, developed over a period of time with a relatively well-defined purpose.

The cause of the insecurity of income is the materialisation of a risk that may be physiological (e.g. accident, illness, old age) or social (e.g. family care, of unemployment). Human society has always looked for ways through which to secure the means of existence of its individual members. As a result of a long historical evolution, social insurance has become the main form of provision against different risks, based on the idea of mandatory pooling of resources of individual citizens to provide benefits in case of need.

## Institutional predecessors of social insurance

A historical search for predecessors of social insurance leads us back to at least five different sources representing institutionalised actions aimed at guaranteeing some material security to specific groups of people.

### Rewards for services

The first and probably the most ancient form of such an action is reward for services that are rendered to holders of political power in society. This would include the distribution of booty to soldiers and the grants of land and pensions to veterans, or to widows and orphans of soldiers killed in wars, as practised in ancient Rome.

In the same category would be the provisions made by different rulers to those who served their interests and helped them in expanding their territories. Such an example would be found in the first social provisions known in post-Columbian Latin America under the designation of '*instituciones graciables*', introduced by the Spanish kings for the benefit of the invading armies and later on for all the king's administrators and members of their families (Moles, 1962, pp 33-55).

In more recent times we can find a similar motivation behind social measures taken for the benefit of civil servants. The history of civil service pensions in Britain, which started towards the end of the 17th century with the provisions for customs officers, soon found its accomplishment in the enactment of a general superannuation scheme for the whole of the civil service. One of the main reasons behind this development was to reward the employee for loyal service and to provide for the decline of his earning capacity (Raphael, 1957).

## The maxim of charity

Another institutional root is found in actions motivated by the religious postulate of charity. Far from being confined to any particular part of the world, the maxim of charity was common to most of the great religions and recommended by them for its own intrinsic value. It should be noted that even the pagan society of ancient Rome found room for charity in the preaching of the moralists.

In the early Christian period, the practice of charity became of paramount importance, since eternal life was to be its reward. The early Christian church itself functioned as a vast organisation for the distribution of charity and the property of the church was considered as a depositary of resources to serve charitable purposes.

At a later stage, monasteries and various religious orders assumed different charitable duties, for instance, redeeming slaves, helping the poor, the sick and strangers, protecting pilgrims and building bridges, in other words, by providing social services to meet specific needs of that period. It can be said that, by and large, the charitable action of the Middle Ages was oriented to help those who fell through the loopholes of the feudal society's system of rights and duties.

## Mutual aid

The third source of institutional activity, which comes very close to that of social insurance, is found in the principle of mutual aid. Funeral and sickness benefit societies were known in ancient Greece and became so popular with the Romans that a special legislation had to be adopted by Marcus Aurelius (AD 161-180) to control them.

The appearance of the medieval guilds coincided with the emergence of towns and handicrafts. The mutual benefit function of occupational fraternities is emphasised more particularly with regard to people in certain dangerous occupations, such as miners and sailors, whose feeling of insecurity is more acute than that of others.

The rural population is in no way behind in this development. It is known that local friendly societies, companies and brotherhoods, most of them of a religious nature, 'abounded in the English villages of the 14th and 15th century ... giving alms, and sometimes regular pensions to members who had fallen into distress' (Webb and Webb, 1927, p 19).

By the time of the Industrial Revolution in Western Europe the mutual benefit societies had made such an advance in their evolution that they became open to all who wished to avail themselves of their services. Simultaneously, mutual benefit activities of trades unions were developed into an important branch of provisions against extreme poverty.

## Occupational welfare

The fourth clearly distinguishable channel of social protection leading to compulsory social insurance is what we now refer to as occupational welfare, which has its roots in the mutual benefit activity of guilds and workers' brotherhoods. Public authority stepped in at an early stage – in the mining industry in Germany as from the middle of the 16th century – to compel the employer to contribute to workers' provident funds. In the second half of the 19th century, legislation on workmen's compensation funds established the principle of the employer's liability for accidents at work. However, in many cases, and independently of any legislative action, employers spontaneously provided for their employees in respect of certain risks.

In Britain, public utilities such as the railways and the gas industry were the first to follow the example of the welfare provisions for the civil service and to establish provident funds and pension schemes. The movement eventually reached other branches of industry, impelled partly by the social feeling of certain employers, and partly by their wish to attract through industrial welfare provisions the most qualified labour. Needless to say, the bargaining power of trades unions was another important element in this development.

Particular mention should be made of the fact that one of the major branches of social security, that is, family allowances, which appeared in France at the end of the 19th century, is clearly of industrial welfare origin.

## Social assistance

Another major historical source of social security is social assistance, which refers to any action of public authorities designed to help the destitute citizen. Its early manifestations took the form of distribution of public money or food by the holders of political power, essentially in order to gain the popular vote and prevent social disorders. The rulers of the city states of ancient Greece, as much as those of the medieval feudal states, considered it necessary to spend part of their resources for this purpose.

However, the early institutional development of social assistance took place mainly at the municipal level. This may be for technical reasons – an efficient organisation of public assistance through a central power requires special administrative machinery, which was missing in most countries. With the progressive decline of feudal society, the increase in the number of indigent people began to constitute a menace to the prosperity of free towns.

The first theory of social assistance was written for the citizens of Bruges, by Jean Louis Vives, in his book *De Subventione Pauperum*, published in 1526 (Monnier, 1856). His work contains a review of existing poor relief provisions, with recommendations as to how to improve them and how to make them more equitable. His idea of social assistance was that of an action based on social solidarity, thought indispensable in view of the mutual interdependence of all human beings in society. Far from being new, this concept marked a great advance in the history of social assistance, particularly since it appeared in a period that considered poverty as a crime against society.

Nevertheless, as shown when the above plan was first applied at Ypres, the very idea of improvement of social assistance at the municipal level contained a seed of its own destruction: the better the poor relief a municipality offered, the more destitute people were drawn to it from other regions, thus causing its ultimate breakdown. Eventually, it became obvious that any defensive action against the continuing spread of destitution that had its roots in the general state of society had to be undertaken at the national level.

In general, social assistance provisions in Western Europe in the 17th and 18th centuries presented a general pattern of cooperation between the central government and the local authorities. In England, the Poor Law of 1601 institutionalised what the Webbs called 'the relief of destitution in the framework of repression' (Webb and Webb, 1927) and remained in force throughout that period. Under this law, local officials were appointed to collect special taxes and use the proceeds to provide work for the destitute and to give relief to disabled people. Towards the end of the 17th century, the first workhouses were set up to serve more as deterrents to the poor rather than as centres of relief. It was not until the end of the 19th century that public opinion, faced with the evidence of facts brought out by systematic research into social causes of poverty (Rowntree, 1899; Booth, 1903), began to admit that an individual could become destitute through no fault of their own.

France maintained a particularly complex structure of social assistance through a network of charitable offices set up for this purpose, and through a variety of penal institutions of forced labour, hospitals and asylums of all kinds. Nevertheless, it was the French Revolution that gave birth to a new doctrine of social assistance in the 'Report of the Committee on the Extinction of Mendicity', published in 1789 (Monnier, 1856). The report recognised the right of every human being to the means of subsistence and described it as a duty of the state to provide work for every citizen. But it considered that work was the only means of assistance that the state should offer, for the state had no practical possibility of distinguishing between deserved and undeserved poverty.

In Germany, the recognition that it was the duty of the state to take care of the undeservedly poor was embodied in the General Law of Prussia of 1794. The obligation to grant assistance to the needy was imposed on local authorities and on the existing corporations. From 1849, local authorities could enforce the creation of occupational provident funds both for artisans and for factory workers. But it was only five years later that a law was passed introducing obligatory participation of workers in the provident funds of the mines and foundries, fixing the minimum benefits for sickness, invalidity and survivors, and for funeral expenses. Some time later, regulations were issued to govern the division of participants into classes and the scheme was given a limited degree of self-administration. The country was firmly on the way towards developing a general social insurance scheme.

## The coming of social insurance

The above description of the institutional predecessors of social insurance is far from exhaustive. Thus, for instance, it should also include private insurance, which has to be developed and assimilated by society before it can be transformed into social insurance. However, a full analysis of these institutional predecessors is beyond the scope of the present text.

It is easy to see that a great deal of overlapping occurred in the course of the historical evolution of the predecessors of social insurance – the principle of reward for services was mixed with occupational welfare, charity with public assistance, and even public assistance with mutual aid. But whatever the mix, there was one constant line that guided this development: the increasing awareness of public authorities of their responsibility for the maintenance of innocent victims of ill fortune.

The currents of thought that eventually give birth to a social institution are like rivers – they usually have several identifiable sources. In the case of social insurance there seems to exist a general consensus that the father of the idea was Daniel Defoe (1660-1731), the world-renowned author of *Robinson Crusoe*. This unusual personality, described by *The Cambridge History of English and American Literature* as an 'embryo sociologist', hardly conforms to the image of a forerunner of social progress. Brought up to become a protestant preacher, he got fervently engaged in politics, fought against King James II and lost his cause as a supporter of William of Orange. He then became a merchant adventurer engaged in overseas trade, went bankrupt and eventually landed himself in prison. When released, he left London for Bristol to keep out of the way. It was there that he wrote *An Essay Upon Projects*, published in 1697.[1]

This little book, inspired by the changes taking place in English society at the end of the 17th century, offered to the new government under William III a series of proposals concerning different social and economic measures, related mostly to the maritime life of the country. We can find there, among others, ideas regarding banking activities, private insurance and friendly societies. It is in this last chapter that the author proposes the generalisation of the idea of friendly societies, as practised among sailors or soldiers, to all groups of the population at risk. 'So mankind must be sorted into classes, and as their contingencies differ, every different sort may be a society upon even terms.'

Of particular interest is the justification of this proposal:

> To argue against the lawfulness of this would be to cry down
> common equity as well as charity; for as it is kind that my
> neighbour should relieve me if I fall into distress or decay,
> so it is but equal he should do so if I agreed to have done
> the same for him – and if God Almighty has commanded
> us to relieve and help one another in distress, surely it must
> be commendable to bind ourselves by agreement to obey
> that command. Nay, it seems to be a project that we are
> led to by the divine rule, and has such a latitude in it that

all the disasters in the world might be prevented by it, and mankind secured from all the miseries, indigences, and distress that happen in the world.[2]

We thus note that a notion of 'common equity' (or shall we say 'social justice'?) joined the principle of mutual aid and charity to pave the way for social insurance. Nevertheless, in spite of the evocation of the divine rule, British parliamentarians did not consider it opportune to approve the first legislative projects concerning the introduction of social insurance, either in 1772 or in 1786. It was hence only a century later that a certain Bismarck launched the first scheme in another country.

The adoption of the first social insurance laws in Germany in the early 1880s was preceded by a series of progressive steps marking the institutional maturation of the new technique. As regards provision against sickness, left in the hands of a multitude of mutual benefit funds, a law on registration adopted in 1876 introduced more uniformity into their administration. As for protection against accidents, this was based originally on the principle of the employers' liability for injuries suffered in the course of work and not imputable to the workers' personal fault. A legislation concerning responsibility of the railways for persons and goods transported was extended to cover their employees already in 1838 and further reinforced in 1869. In 1871, a law on employers' responsibility for accidents was made to cover the railways, mines, quarries and factories, and in 1878 it was further extended to textile mills, construction and agriculture. This legislation was naturally followed by the creation of ad hoc insurance companies.

When in 1881 Bismarck announced in the Emperor's message to the Reichstag his intention to create general compulsory social insurance schemes, considerable administrative experience in the field of sickness and accident insurance was already available. From among the remaining risks, which he was pledged to cover, only old-age and invalidity insurance had to be built from the start. The legislation on sickness insurance was adopted in 1883, on accident insurance in 1884, and on old-age and invalidity insurance in 1889.

Similar developments took place in Britain where 30 years later Lloyd George embodied the principle of social insurance in the National Insurance Act of 1911. The sickness insurance scheme enacted under this legislation, alongside with unemployment insurance, was presented as an effort to generalise the work of trades unions and friendly societies with help from the state. At the administrative level, the application of the formula of 'approved societies' opened the door to commercial industrial assurance companies.

From the historical angle, it would thus appear that the introduction of a nationwide social insurance scheme occurred at a time when several institutional predecessors of social insurance were sufficiently well established to be 'nationalised', or, at any rate, to serve as a basis for the development of an administrative platform for the new scheme.

There is far less similarity when it comes to the question of political opportunity for introducing a scheme. It has been generally admitted that in Bismarck's Germany the main motive behind this step was the government's wish to break the dynamics of the revolutionary socialist movement of that time. Social insurance, based on the idea of cooperation between the state, the employer and the worker,[3] was seen by many as a symbol of state socialism, designated to split the ranks of the working class in its struggle for power in society.

In the British case, the situation was in many respects different. The political stage for the introduction of social insurance was prepared by a landslide electoral victory of the Liberal Party in 1906. This gave a particular orientation to the discussions of the Royal Commission on the Poor Laws, which took place between the years 1905 and 1909, and made a great impact on the public opinion of the country. The opposition to the bismarckian state socialism was still present in the attitude of the newly created Labour Party, which, although originally in favour of the social programme of the Liberal Party, was deeply split on the issue of social insurance, in contrast to trades unions, which were generally in favour. The political challenge for the Liberal Party consisted in the large popular vote, which imposed the acceptance of certain obligations on its leaders. In the opinion of a young liberal politician, named Winston S. Churchill,

> The working classes will not – and indeed they cannot – continue to bear the terrible insecurity of their lives. A minimum level of wages, an effective form of insurance against sickness, unemployment and old age – these are the questions, which will dominate the life of political parties in the future. (Cormack, 1953)

Accordingly, the liberals had to make a decisive step towards the social protection of the working population by adopting a new formula intended to provide help to lower-paid workers through employer and state contributions, without the stigma of poor relief.

The interest in social insurance was general all over Europe and intensive activity regarding the study of its ideology and techniques was noticeable both at the national and international level throughout the final decades of the 19th century. However, the introduction of the corresponding legislation was dependent on the political situation in each country. Central Europe under the rule of the old Austro-Hungarian monarchy was much slower in this respect than Bismarck's Germany due essentially to its political instability and the strength of its socialist movement opposing social insurance for earlier-mentioned ideological reasons. In France, the first law on workers' and peasants' pensions, adopted in 1910, was never implemented and it was not until 1930 that a new legislation could get off to a start. Different countries followed different ways to introduce their social insurance schemes according to the conditions of their political and socioeconomic environment. The next mutation in the development of the institution took place during the Second World War, when the experience of wartime social solidarity prepared the political ground for moving another step ahead.

## The road to social security

There are many views on the origins or the first use of the term 'social security'.[4] The most frequently quoted forerunner is the Social Security Act of 1935, adopted in the US. However, this concerns social insurance legislation covering only old-age and survival benefits for wage-earners.

The first integrated social security system in the Western world was set up three years later in New Zealand. Similar to major legislative advances in other countries,

> the Social Security Act of 1938 was not an entirely fresh departure. It built on established ground. The principle of universal contribution for unemployment benefits had been established in 1930. The principle of old age pensions had been established in 1898; and nearly all the other services had been foreshadowed to some degree before 1938. (Mendelsohn, 1954, p 182)

But the New Zealand system had some specific features: with the exception of several universal benefits (family allowances, superannuation, medical benefits) it was not a true universal social insurance scheme. Although financed partially by means of ad hoc contributions, it did not take them into account when deciding on eligibility for benefits – this depended entirely on a means test. In this scheme even the notion of 'contribution' is blurred so that many authors prefer to speak about financing out of general revenue by means of an earmarked tax.[5]

The outbreak of the Second World War put an end to the gradual expansion of social insurance[6] until the launch of the Beveridge Report (Beveridge, 1942). The circumstances of this major historical event merit a closer examination. In 1941, William Beveridge, a liberal politician and well-known expert on unemployment insurance, was appointed head of an interdepartmental committee, set up by the government 'to undertake, with special reference to the inter-relation of the schemes, a survey of the existing national schemes of social insurance and allied services, and to make recommendations' (Beveridge, 1942, p 2). Published in 1942, the report in itself was 'a technical analysis of the problems and methods of social insurance, with some drastic and often very ingenious proposals for unifying the whole system and making it simpler and more efficient' (Marshall, 1965, p 76). But Beveridge was a man of vision – the government requested him to make a survey of social insurance and he came back with a plan for social security. As he pointed out at the end of his report, 'statement of a reconstruction policy by a nation at war is statement of the uses to which that nation means to put victory, when victory is achieved' (Beveridge, 1942, para 459).

The government was not inclined to give his report more importance than was originally intended and the personal attitude of the Prime Minister Winston Churchill to him was highly critical. But 'there came a dramatic change when the Minister of Information, Bernard Bracken, had a look at the Report. He saw at once that it was magnificent material for export to all the world, and a weapon of first importance against Hitler' (Beveridge, 1954). There can hardly be any doubt that it was this Ministry's sustained effort that turned the Beveridge Report into a powerful image of the new world people fought for and into a peacetime objective for many nations. The radio and press campaign provoked such a reaction in the British public that the government had to give up its hesitation as to the follow-up to be given to the document – hesitation that, in the opinion of many observers, paved the way to the 1945 electoral victory of the Labour Party. Thanks to the incessant broadcast of the BBC, the whole world was ready to move in the direction shown by the Beveridge Report and was confirmed in the objectives the International Labour Organization (ILO) adopted in the Philadelphia Declaration of 1944.

The post-war years saw an extraordinary expansion of social security schemes all over the world and the establishment of the welfare state in most industrialised countries of Western Europe. The economic growth that took place during the first post-war decades provided a basis for a continuing advance in the coverage of social needs and the development of adequate social welfare policies became a political imperative in Western democracies. The conviction that an ongoing rapid economic growth was a permanent feature of societal evolution became so strong that nobody seriously thought about a possible reverse in this trend and about the need for linking the growing volume of social transfers and vested rights to the performance of national economies. This situation was perpetuated by other positive factors such as full employment, helping to keep income from contributions and social spending at a desirable level, and the capacity of governments to remain in control and steer their national economy. With respect to international politics, the dynamics of this development was sustained by the communist countries boasting about the superiority of social guarantees enjoyed by their populations. Although the price to be paid for this kind of social protection was a matter of common knowledge, the Western capitalist system had to maintain a reasonable level of social welfare in order to be credible.

## The beginning of retrenchment

The first oil shock of 1973 spelled the end of the period of expansion of the welfare state. The belief in a permanently high economic growth was deeply shattered and governments started to grapple with the difficulty of satisfying growing needs in the presence of diminishing resources. Among the defenders of the welfare state, nobody was prepared to consider a reduction of benefits at a time when they were most needed. Hence the resistance to any major revision of the existing schemes and a call for rationalisation and simplification of welfare transfers. But the second oil crisis in 1979 and subsequent developments clearly indicated that there was not going to be a way back.

The most direct impact of the reduced economic growth was revealed in the steep increase in unemployment, the only really 'social' risk covered by the existing schemes of social security, as distinct from physiological risks of human existence such as sickness or accident. During the first years after the onset of economic difficulties, social security schemes of most countries tried to face the challenge by helping the unemployed through easier access to benefits granted under other branches of social insurance, such as invalidity or old age. Fortunately, before this rather understandable reaction to mass unemployment could ruin the whole system of social security financing, governments had been able to recall the old lesson taught by Beveridge, that social security schemes were not meant to combat large-scale unemployment. They recognised that unlike structural unemployment, the former was a major disease of the economic system of society and had to be dealt with primarily by economic and other systemic measures rather than by social welfare benefits.[7]

Other factors reinforced the pressure on the existing social security systems. With the onset of globalisation, governments started losing control of the parameters governing their economic policies and sought ways of increasing their competitiveness in the international markets; in this respect, a reduction in the cost of labour became one of the most obvious targets. At the same time, new demographic trends began to modify the age structure of the population, with a considerable impact on the cost of public pension schemes.

It was at this juncture that democratic countries witnessed the collapse of the communist world, provoking a dangerous illusion on the part of many supporters of the capitalist system that this implosion of the collectivist totalitarian regimes was due to the superiority of their own ideas regarding solutions to both economic and social problems of society. It is hardly surprising that this moment was considered propitious for a major ideological attack against the welfare state led by the World Bank with considerable potential power to introduce changes in social welfare systems of many countries in all continents (World Bank, 1994).[8]

The ideological war launched by the supporters of the neoliberal school of thought was surprising on account of the vehemence and nature of the arguments used, often outside the terms of reference of an expert debate on the subject. Thus, it was strange to see a serious international organisation accusing social security of having failed to prevent the extension of poverty – as if anybody ever pretended that the institution was able to do more than to act on a limited number of causes of poverty. Obviously, after the years of frustration and suppressed criticism, when nobody dared to attack head on the flourishing and politically correct welfare state, the opportunity was too good to be missed. But the debate did not move an inch from where it had been many years ago: the neoliberal thinking found no room for accommodating the concept of social insurance based on the notion of solidarity among citizens. It was hence reduced to a monologue expressing belief in a different world from the one that gave birth to social security.

The World Bank maintained for some time a considerable impact on pension scheme reforms in developing and transition countries, but soon its policy was put to the test as it came to grips with reality. The result was a severe criticism voiced from inside the organisation when Orszak and Stiglitz (1999) suggested that a privately managed defined contribution system may not always be the best solution for the second pension pillar and that a country may well consider adopting a public defined benefit plan. The statement was based on the recognition that a number of factors, for example the quality of financial institutions in a country, may determine the outcome of the model favoured by the World Bank. As for the industrialised countries of the Western world, they never took the plan very seriously, as it did not come anywhere close to what could constitute a politically acceptable solution to their old-age pension problems. The suggestion to confine social security in old age to private financial markets was subsequently ruled out of the realm of serious social policy options with the burst of the speculative bubble in the opening years of the 21st century, providing a most timely demonstration of the risks involved in the World Bank's proposals.

Throughout the period of the neoliberal campaign against the welfare state, many specialists were puzzled by the fact that in spite of the rhetoric used in academic and governmental circles, there were only a few signs of any serious retrenchment of the welfare state. This was being explained by various considerations, such as dependence on backward looking statistical series, or simply by political resilience of the institution. Others, however, pointed out that in certain industrialised countries a number of small piecemeal reforms were taking place, adding up to a qualitative reform and possibly to a systemic change of the welfare state (Cox, 1998). In more recent years, suggestion was made that the apparent stability and resilience may be due to the use of quantitative methods of research predominant in cross-national comparative studies of the response of welfare states to existing pressures, which tend to overemphasise this phenomenon, as against modifications and change. On the other hand, case studies of the policy-making process in individual countries tend to provide a stronger focus on the role of politics in the changing institutional framework, which may be opening the way to substantial restructuring. In this way, after the interregnum of two closing decades of the previous century, a 'silver age' may now succeed the 'golden age' of the welfare state: citizen welfare remains a major objective of policy, but is tempered by concerns about international competitiveness, cost constraints and individual choice (Taylor-Gooby, 2002).

This vision of a progressive adaptation of social security institutions to the gradual reduction of economic growth, plausible in the closing years of the preceding millennium, has now been deeply shattered by two successive disruptions of international financial and economic functions.

There does not seem to be any time left for progressive adjustments since the economic disorder and sudden global impoverishment menace the very existence of social institutions organically linked to the production of wealth. If the existing capitalist market machinery finds its way back to another spell of continuing growth, the chances are that those successful individuals who regain prosperity will fully embrace the neoliberal credo and its preference for social assistance measures for the weak. But if the comeback is slow and socially painful, it is likely to provoke revolutionary movements and attempts to overthrow the existing social and economic order. Whatever the case may be, it seems evident that a major reappraisal of existing trends in social security policy is needed to bring the institution into the front line of defence of a socially just and democratic society.

## Notes

[1] For the full text of the book and all quotations in the following paragraphs, see the *Electronic Text Collection* of the University of Adelaide, Australia. htpp//ebooks.adelaide.edu.au/d/defoe/daniel/d31es/

[2] It is worth noting that in this context Daniel Defoe drove his imagination even further so as to envisage for social insurance the future role of the United Nations: 'First general peace might be secured all over the world by it, if all the powers agreed to suppress him that usurped or encroached upon his neighbour....'

[3] In reality, with regard to pensions, Bismarck himself had not intended that the employees should be obliged to contribute. But when the Act was passed he was no longer in power, and by then all the machinery for compulsory insurance had been created to deal with sickness and accidents, and could be used for pensions (Dawson, 1912, pp 14-19).

[4] The term was used in a more general sense by Simon Bolivar in his speech known as 'Discurso de Angostura' delivered on 15 February 1819. Discussing an ideal democratic system for an independent Latin America, he said: 'the most perfect system of government is that which results in the greatest sum of happiness, the greatest sum of social security and the greatest sum of political stability' (see Jorge Nunez: 'Un hombre llamado Simon Bolivar', www.simon-bolivar.org).

[5] At the outset, this contribution represented an annual registration fee plus a one-shilling charge on each pound of income from whatever source.

[6] This would not be true about Latin America where several countries introduced social insurance schemes with the help of the ILO whose headquarters had been transferred temporarily to Montreal.

[7] This at least is the implication of the concept exposed by Beveridge himself several years after the publication of his report: 'Social security, as conceived in the Beveridge Report, is security organised or assisted by the State against those risks to which the individual will remain exposed, even when the condition of society as a whole is as good as it can be. Social security on this definition excludes measures of general application for improving the condition of society – full employment, minimum wages, factory laws, public health, housing, education and so forth' (Lord Beveridge in Robson, 1948, 'Epilogue').

[8] The World Bank pension plan is analysed in more detail in Chapter Two under 'Social security and neoliberalism'.

# TWO

# Essential issues of social protection in our society

The message of the brief history of social security developments worldwide that were reviewed in the previous chapter is fairly clear: the social security institution is in danger and steps should be taken to prevent its progressive institutional dismantlement. What is at stake is not only the preservation of its chief functions regarding the security of existence of the individual but also the preservation of some of the basic values of the society we live in. The call for a major institutional reform with a view to safeguarding social security should be logically accompanied by an effort to clarify the main issues involved in its current operations. This chapter is intended to provide some guidance in this respect.

## Social security in a globalised world: the changing environment

According to the estimates emanating from the International Labour Office and quoted in several of its publications, only some 20-30% of the total world population have access to meaningful social security cash benefits; the remaining 70-80% live in conditions of social insecurity, in spite of the progress of human rights. These figures indicate the magnitude of the problem the world has to face at present and the deep gap that separates the developing world from the old industrialised countries.

There seems to be, as part of the general impact of globalisation, a move in favour of an overall coordination of social policies. Through the institutional network of international organisations monitoring the globalisation process, a political commitment is being created calling for expansion of social protection and its extension to the rural sector and informal economy. But this is not a simple task since for the vast majority of the rural population in a developing country the very concept of income replacement has little meaning. Furthermore, not all rural societies have the same social needs and the process of developing adequate methods of social protection may require heavy financial investments. The global interdependence of social policies thus adds another dimension to the difficulties of adaptation of social security to the conditions of the 21st century.

Another important change is being felt in the everyday life of Western societies: people are growing older. According to current estimates, about 15 years have been added to the average length of human life over the last 50 years. This is obviously of fundamental importance not only for old-age protection but also for other risks related to old age, such as long-term sickness or disability. The first natural reaction to this good news would be to add the additional lifetime to the period of retirement – but this may be difficult to realise in view of the effect on the cost of pensions. And since somebody will have to pay, it seems indispensable to create new sources of finance and seek a new retirement pattern; for instance, after the period of full economic activity during the productive age, people should be given the possibility to engage first in a socially useful and remunerated activity before taking full retirement in the post-productive age. We may only hope to be able to avoid any major social conflicts during the transition period to this new long-life society.

The changing socioeconomic conditions that shape social security developments over the years also produce a new political climate that constitutes the most immediate determining factor of its evolution. The previous chapter dealt at some length with the story of the neoliberal attack on the fundamental concept of social security in the middle of the 1990s, followed by a more evenly balanced attitude in more recent years. But is this moderate approach likely to prevail at the grassroots level with people having some role to play in the economic life of Western societies? Direct observation of current discussions in many European countries makes it difficult to give an affirmative answer to this question.

While the international leaders of the neoliberal movement may show a more reconciling attitude, different actors in the national economy seem to be far from retreating from their positions, engaged as they are in maintaining the economic viability of their enterprises. In their daily struggle for survival they may not always perceive the violent reactions that the absence of a reasonable social policy provokes on the part of their opponents.[1] We thus witness a progressive radicalisation of the positions on the left of the political spectrum that strongly reminds some members of the older generation of the time when they had the ill fortune to experience the advent of communism in their countries. Should the move towards a rapid reform of the existing social security system fail to produce some tangible results, the old battle against the capitalist system may start again. It is likely to take place independently of the fact that the experience of social security under the communist regimes in the previous century was far from convincing.

## The changing content of social security and limits of income redistribution

The astonishing expansion of social security during the post-war years was due to a spontaneous growth responding to the sentiment of extreme insecurity during wartime. However, to the extent that different national approaches to the problem of securing human existence in society resulted in the adoption of different systems, it became extremely difficult to develop a common concept of the welfare state and of a corresponding social policy.

We can recall in this context difficulties experienced by international experts whenever the question was raised of defining, even in general terms, the objectives, the structure and the functions of social security. Historically, the foundations of an international concept of social security were laid in the Declaration of Philadelphia of 1944, the new charter of the ILO for the post-war period. But the real task of defining the institution was undertaken in the ILO Convention on Minimum Norms of Social Security of 1952. It is worth noting that, notwithstanding the enormous developments in the subsequent decades, definitions contained in this document have remained until today the reference for anybody faced with the formidable task of describing the institution and its functions. For many people, only a pragmatic approach to defining what has come under the scope of social security could make any sense.[2]

It should be noted in this context that in Europe there has never been a common concept of the welfare state. Thus, for instance, the British insistence on social security being an integral part of the rights of citizenship was never properly understood across the Channel. For a number of reasons, throughout the history of the French social protection system, the state never played a decisive role in providing security of existence for its citizens and was not even expected or trusted to be able to do so. Social security came through the progress of social rights of working people and became very distinctly a political achievement of the left, logically accompanied by the participation of protected persons in the administration of the institution.

But Britain started changing the content of its social security system in a relatively short time after its enactment. The principles of equality and social justice embodied in universal social rights did not really cover the same objectives as the principle of social insurance. Nor was the British system apt to follow improved standards of living and to increase levels of protection in the same degree. As it happened, within two decades after the adoption of the Beveridge Report, its main ideas – that is, universality, flat-rate contributions and flat-rate benefits – were falling short of the needs of a prosperous society with different requirements for different social classes. Thus, while the unification of social risks within one system was never really achieved, as a result of the application of flat-rate contributions and benefits, 'for most of the middle classes social security became only a small and unnoticed top up to their major provision which came through tax-subsidised employers' schemes or private insurance' (Abel–Smith, 1992, p 17).

The process of the changing content was also influenced by the internal inconsistencies of the Beveridge scheme combining the universality of social rights of citizenship with the contractual principle inherent in social insurance. If the grant of a social benefit was due strictly on the ground of citizenship, there was no need for an ad hoc contribution for this purpose (Baldwin, 1992, p 35).[3] The insistence of Beveridge on the contributory principle reflected in fact the reluctance of the British citizen to depend on society for any 'free' handouts, and the citizen's preference for a contractual arrangement under which the benefit is granted as of right in return for a contribution. The emphasis was hence on self-help and self-reliance rather than on a right to benefit on the strength of citizenship. With these considerations Beveridge manifestly introduced into his concept moral attitudes, which distinguish social security systems from mechanical redistribution of income through public taxation measures.

Among the countries that followed the road of the expanding welfare state, France developed a system closely linked to employment and largely reflecting the division of the population into different occupational groups. This did not prevent one of its leading social security experts, writing in the early 1950s, to state that the purpose of social security was:

> to transfer the income from individuals and social groups advantaged by birth, fortune or success in accumulating material wealth, to those who are in need. Social security policy undoubtedly aims at compensating victims of risks, but it wants above all to remove inequalities between individuals and social classes. (Durand, 1953, p 292)

This was clearly the expression of a political credo, a direct resonance of the period between the First and Second World War when social insurance was an integral part of the programme of all social democratic parties.

It appeared, however, that income redistribution, so ardently desired by those wishing to use social security for other than risk protection purposes, did not always work in the desired direction. After closer scrutiny, the income transfers operated by social security revealed great variations between different branches of activity or between different groups of the population. The income redistribution was shown to depend entirely on the mechanism used to finance social security expenditure and also on the way a specific group of the population would set about to fully exploit a social security scheme. Due to better education, and hence more at ease in handling sometimes fairly complex administrative procedures, the middle classes were found to be better equipped than the low-income classes to take advantage of social security benefits.

Income redistribution is a measure of public policy for dealing with inequalities of human existence and is often considered as an objective in itself. Its chief institutional channel is the system of the imposition of taxes payable to a public authority to finance collective provisions for members of a community. The fact that taxes are fixed in relation to the income or property of the individual indicates the presence of a social aspect of taxation, but it does not transform fiscal into social policy. Income redistribution is essentially an instrument of fiscal and not of social policy and the fact that it is often the result of the application of certain social policy measures, such as social insurance, does not modify the primary purpose of these measures. The basic idea of social insurance is the pooling of resources among members of a given community, so as to make it possible to help those who fall victim to a physiological or social risk. To the extent that the materialisation of these risks is generally independent of the will of the individual, it is also an instrument of social justice.

When the notion of social risk is extended to also cover the situation of low income or other circumstances leading to an inferior position in society, the concept of social insurance is transformed into the redistribution of income in favour of weaker members of society. It is undoubtedly at this point that ideology steps in and takes advantage of the changing dynamics of the societal environment. Understandable as it may be, this process, nevertheless, raises the question of the finality or the raison d'être of social insurance in society, and – to the extent that institutions are supposed to last only as long as they remain true to the ideas that presided over their origins – the question of long-term sustainability of social insurance as a social institution. The danger that lies in confusing the two policy instruments is fairly evident: in the period of an economic crisis, when a majority of citizens comes to the conclusion that the existing redistribution of income is excessive and undesirable, the insurance function of the respective institutional channel tends to be cut at the same time. This menace is very much with us at the present time.

Several factors are at work to facilitate this confusion. In times of prosperity, the difference in objectives is not readily noticeable and does not warrant a special effort to keep insisting on it. But when the taxation system of a country is overstretched, it becomes too tempting for the authorities to transfer some of its burden to social insurance contributions, which are more readily accepted by the population. Furthermore, when a country has a social security system run and financed by the state, the difference between taxes and social security contributions becomes for many practical purposes undistinguishable, as shown in the current practice of many Anglo-Saxon countries.

Although social security systems in Western Europe show at present a remarkable resilience to outside economic pressures, the continuing trend towards the limitation of social expenditure, sustained by low economic growth, is likely to continue. This situation will invite further attacks against the existing social insurance structures demanding complete dismantlement of these systems and their replacement by social assistance or private arrangements. Given the weakening appeal of the postulate of citizens' solidarity and the growing distrust of the younger generation regarding the capacity of collective state systems to ensure the security of their existence, this continuing pressure could seriously damage social welfare structures for many decades to come.

The only way of averting this danger is to return to the origins of social security, in the sense of assigning to social insurance its basic function of securing human existence against those physiological and social risks, to which – in line with the Beveridge concept mentioned in the previous chapter – the individual will be exposed even when general conditions of society are as good as they can be. This policy should leave to the taxation system the role of income redistribution, according to the political will of the population; it would have the advantage of reinforcing the foundations of social security and enable the institution to assume fully its normal functions. It should help, at the same time, to do away with the concept of redistribution as an invasive act of public authority limiting individual freedom, while retaining the concept of providing resources needed for public services, in line with the citizens' capacity to contribute.

## The global economic trap of human rights

Our somewhat pessimistic view of the future of the welfare state is based on the perspective of a relatively low economic growth in occidental societies for a long time to come. Some may object to this and say that the development of the world economy is unpredictable and that a sudden positive change in our economic destinies may turn the clock back and ease the pressure. However, while high growth situations are likely to occur in many countries half way up the scale of economic development, this is unlikely to happen in old industrialised countries sharing the philosophy of the market economy, democracy and human rights.

In the period of the globalisation of exchanges, the above 'free world principles' cannot but lead to a progressive decline of industrialised countries by the simple fact of the long-term levelling out of wages and standards of living between them and the low-cost developing countries. Any attempt to slow down this process is bound to hurt the economic principles of free trade and free circulation of labour on one side, and the political imperative of the advancement of human rights on the other. The open advocates of a controlled development, preserving a 'soft landing' of the prevailing world order, or those wishing to stop the rush of poor immigrants from the South to the North, will be a priori ruled out as being 'politically incorrect' and will have little chance of success.

This manifest and yet hardly avowable contradiction between the market economy and human rights philosophy, which has now been revealed by globalisation, goes back to the early declarations of human rights; their authors simply forgot to ask about the economic cost of their ideal to society – as if any such concept could fail to have an economic counterpart. Admittedly, in their time, the economic dimension of social phenomena was not an object of daily preoccupations. And yet, if the idea of human rights is to have any real meaning, the society adopting it must know how much it is prepared to pay for its general application. It seems at present that out of sheer habit we continue to proclaim these ideals without being in the least ready or capable to cover the cost of their attainment. This also means that we are guilty of deceiving millions who tend to believe in human rights as if they were a reality and behave accordingly.

Coming to terms with this contradiction implies the awareness of the progressive economic decline of the industrialised world and the acceptance of some hard rules that are likely to govern the survival of social protection institutions and more particularly that of social insurance. A new elaboration of the concept of social justice relating to the materialisation of physiological and social risks, and an absolute transparency of monetary transfers operated by any new social security system, seem to be a sine qua non of such survival.

## The problem of the integration of social and economic policies

By their very nature, all major institutions created by society will simultaneously affect several aspects of human activity, because of their interconnection within the societal environment. Thus, for instance, a workers' strike will always have a distinct economic, social and political impact with varying degrees of intensity. Nevertheless, most of the time, there will be a dominant or primary function corresponding to the main purpose of the institution and reflecting the most immediate reasons that led to its creation. The determination of this basic purpose of a social institution is of considerable importance since any confusion in this matter may prove to be detrimental to the continuation of its existence.

Changes in the perception of the main function of an institution may occur either as a result of a change in the respective societal environment, or as a result of successive modifications of the structure and functions of the institution itself. In the case of social security, changes have taken place in both directions. At the societal environment level, the institution was born in the climate of war, which heightened the sense of national solidarity and rendered plausible the fulfilment of the popular aspiration for a guarantee of minimum existence in conditions preserving human dignity. The Beveridge Report responded to this wish by creating the concept of social benefits granted as of right, in virtue of contributions made to a common scheme. In the early stages the global social impact of this measure was probably more important than the economic impact of the benefit. In post–war Britain, the newspapers made it their headlines when the former Field Marshal Montgomery went to the Post Office to claim his first pension benefit; the scheme had demonstrated that everybody was equal before the law and there was no stigma attached to it. The overriding and all-important principle was that of equality of social rights of all citizens.

The primarily social function of social security is derived from the fact that the institution serves the very preservation of individual human existence in society on the ground of social justice. Admittedly, the institution performs a number of economic functions, which are of great importance for the national economy. One of them is precisely the redistribution of income, which is sometimes considered as an end in itself. But this is hardly justifiable since, as we have seen from different historical references, in social security the social function of an income transfer is intrinsically linked to the conditions under which it is made. It is essential to recognise – what many economists tend to forget – that the impact of a grant of £100 from social insurance (this is, benefit as of right fully preserving individual human dignity) is not the same as that of the same amount received from public assistance. The economic effect of a social security measure is only part of the global effect, which consists in providing the individual with satisfactory conditions of life. While it is perfectly legitimate to study economic aspects of social security and to highlight their importance, it would be preposterous to turn the institution – as had been sometimes attempted – into an instrument of economic policy. The simultaneous presence of these two aspects of social reality complicates no doubt a general perception of the global function of the institution – keeping them in balance is possibly one of the greatest challenges of societal governance.

The difficulty of integrating social and economic policies depends to a large extent on the state˜ of the socioeconomic well-being of society. Towards the end of the 1960s, a great deal of effort, especially at the United Nations level, went into the elaboration of a theory of integrated social and economic development for low-income countries. In the Western world, this was accompanied by intensive studies in the field of societal planning based on the development of models and social indicators. The promising advances that had been made came to a halt with the onset of the first oil crises in the middle of the 1970s. Economic considerations acquired the character of political imperatives and social policy came to be implemented under this rule.

In more recent years, the question of the integration of social and economic policy has received a great deal of attention as result of the developments in the European Union (EU). This time, the central issue is how to ensure a reasonable degree of social protection in a community driven essentially by considerations of economic interest. To the extent that the EU has left social questions in the hands of national governments and has not developed any specific social policy of its own, the process consists of a series of confrontations between the economic policy of the EU and social preoccupations of all interested partners. Indeed, it is the variation of tensions between these two poles of interest and an effort to keep them in balance, which is the driving power behind social reforms within the EU (Clotuche, 2005, p 27).

The adoption of an important European treaty known as the Single European Act in 1986 brought the realisation of a great internal market, which was accompanied by a policy of economic and social cohesion. This gave more scope for the social policies of individual member states to play the role of a mechanism of adjustment for dealing with negative aspects of economic integration. In an atmosphere marked by the 'crisis of the welfare state', the debates pointed to the need for adopting two complementary strategies, one to promote the harmonisation of social protection and the other to take up ad hoc measures for the necessary adjustments. Since harmonisation has never been really acceptable to national governments, it is the second line of approach that is mostly followed, under the conditions of growing financial difficulties, raising the question of sustainability of the existing social systems.

The Maastricht Treaty of 1992, which launched the process of coordination of economic policies, has also had a considerable impact on the social policies of individual member states. In the same year, the European Council adopted two recommendations: the first deals with common criteria regarding resources and benefits granted by national social protection systems; the second concerns the convergence of objectives of social protection policies. Many governments will use this invitation to operate changes in their social legislation. This process coincides with the appearance, on the international scene, of the so-called 'Washington consensus', invented by the world financial institutions to guide economic policies for developing countries of Latin America. The accent is placed on the negative effects of redistributive social protection policies.

In the following years, it is the World Bank and the International Monetary Fund (IMF) who dominate the discussions about the new social protection model based essentially on savings and investments in financial markets and on private insurance. The traditional defenders of social security such as the ILO and, in the non-governmental sector, the ISSA, will be reduced to the role of polite opponents without the necessary political weight to change the course of events. This situation will change significantly after the bitter experience and practical demonstration of the catastrophic insecurity of world financial markets of the early 2000s. Meanwhile the EU, having launched its Lisbon strategy in the year 2000, struggles on in its search for integrated social and economic policy. The widely publicised 'open method of coordination', applied also to the social policy sector, has hardly any chance to make much difference. After all, in this field, learning from another's experience and adopting the best has been the rule guiding all activities of many international organisations, and particularly the ISSA, since their foundation.

What are the causes of this situation and why is it so difficult to integrate social and economic policies? In deeper analysis, this difficulty has its roots in the functional duality of an individual in society. The well-being of an individual, who is the basic unit of society, is by definition the supreme aim of all societal activity; but an individual is at the same time an essential unit of economic production and, as such, subject to the laws of the market economy. Equalising the tension between these two poles of human existence is the main driving force behind all social development and its control is one of the chief responsibilities of any democratic government.[4]

Considerable efforts are being made in many quarters to show that certain social policies are favourable to economic development. This is certainly true and in most cases the argument depends on whether we judge the situation from the short- or long-term point of view. But this argumentation is also dangerous since it seems to suggest that certain social policies are good *because* they serve economic development. This way of presentation would inevitably lead to the elimination of social measures that may not be immediately recognised as being economy-friendly or those that are, in short term at least, in direct conflict with economic interests. This reflection brings us back to the question of specific finalities of policies and institutions, which have to be recognised and respected as such. In the last resort, a political decision has to be made in conflicting situations so as to determine which of the competing policies is to be given priority.

## Social security and communism

All students of the history of social security learn that at the beginning there was an opposition to the introduction of social insurance in Bismarck's Germany by the socialist movement. The institution, labelled as an instrument of 'state socialism', was considered as a political expedient meant to pacify the working classes and break their revolutionary spirit.

This position has not changed substantially over the years except in countries where the communists took power. Ten years after the end of the Second World War, it was still possible to read in France that:

> The Communist Party considers that a real social security
> will be achieved only when the capitalist system will have
> disappeared and a socialist society installed, in which work
> will provide for all social needs.... The first condition of
> a real social insurance is that it should be entirely at the

expense of the employer, of whatever kind, and without any worker's contribution. It is the employers who use and abuse the worker's force. (*L'Humanité*, 28 October 1955)

The message is clear: far from being a support of human solidarity and social justice, social insurance is an instrument of class struggle.

The situation is of course totally different when revolution takes place and the individual becomes part of a huge collective enterprise called the state. In return for work, which constitutes a legal obligation, the collective provides, at the basic maintenance level, for all the individual's needs in case of materialisation of a physical risk (by definition, a social risk such as unemployment is not supposed to exist). This type of 'social security' ensures, for a certain period of time at least, a passive acceptance of the new social order while maintaining the health and the working capacity of the labour force.

Most communist regimes established after the Second World War inherited from previous governments nationwide social insurance schemes, which had to be transformed to fit the new model. The transformation normally proceeded in two stages. At the first stage, the system of social insurance contributions was abolished and the financial responsibility for the whole scheme transferred to the state budget; this enabled the regime to claim that social security was provided to all citizens free of charge. The second stage saw the abandonment of the link between the benefit and the qualifying period of insurance and the benefits were made dependent exclusively on the period of employment.

In comparison with the level of wages, and within the socioeconomic parameters of its own closed society, the communist regime probably offered to wage-earners higher benefits and a more complete coverage than any capitalist country could do. The Soviet experts used to claim that with the state taking over responsibility for the whole welfare system, social security as an institution reached the summit of its development. They also considered their concepts to be more advanced than those of the Western world. Thus, for instance, with regard to the equality of men and women, they went far beyond the requirement of equality and adopted the principle of a privileged treatment for women on account of their role in society. This was demonstrated by a policy of granting them a very low retirement age (in many countries as from the age of 53) according to the number of children they had brought up. But all such assertions could stand up only as long as the communist countries could be considered as a self-contained territory detached from the rest of the world. The superiority claim was manifestly gone the moment a comparison was made with the wage-earners' purchasing power and quality of life in Western countries.

For the totalitarian holder of the political power, the new concept of social security obviously contained an invitation to distribute state benefits not so much according to everyone's needs, but according to service rendered to the country. This principle was applied from the initial stages of social security developments in the Soviet Union, when the first to be covered were those employees considered to be most important from the point of view of the build-up of the Soviet state. It is due to this heritage that after the end of the Second World War all Soviet satellites ended up with the division of workers into three categories, each of them having specific qualifying conditions and benefits.[5]

But the policy of privileged treatment with respect to social security benefits also has other applications. Thus, for instance, in the case of professions involving heavy and dangerous work, it may serve as an enticement to attract people to jobs that are positively harmful to their health. The classic example is the uranium mines where relatively poor health protection measures were responsible for extremely high mortality. The same example may also serve to indicate that social benefits have been used at the same time essentially for the attainment of economic goals. This practice was later developed into a whole system of incentives, particularly well organised in the pension field.

Another function attributed to social security benefits was that of reward for especially meritorious services. Thus, for instance, many countries under communist rule introduced what was referred to as 'personal pensions', granted to persons who had a record of distinguished service in the economic, scientific or cultural life of the country and also in national defence, administration and 'other sectors of public activity'. This last-mentioned category of meritorious performance naturally covered, above all, services rendered to the Communist Party.

Not surprisingly, at the opposite end of the reward for services is a denial of benefit in the case of the social misbehaviour of the worker. A typical example comes from the former Czechoslovakia, where one day of unauthorised or unexplained absence from work was sanctioned by a withdrawal of family allowances for the next month.

A special mention should also be made of particular functions devolved to workmen's compensation. The monumental upheaval that had wiped out all private enterprises and instituted in their place one omnipotent employer – the state – modified profoundly the philosophy of this branch. While before the revolution the distasteful private employer had to be fought and burdened with the full cost of accident compensation, the new benevolent state-employer had to be protected against the misbehaviour of some employees and helped in order to secure the desired productivity of its enterprise. However, it did not take long for political leaders to realise that the new system was not quite adapted to social reality. While enterprises actually financed the whole social security system through levies operated by the state, they were not directly concerned by the expenditure side of accident insurance relating to medical treatment, rehabilitation or invalidity pensions, all provided or paid for by different state services. This naturally led to negligence in the application of occupational health and safety measures. Consequently, in order to make enterprises behave more responsibly, the accident insurance scheme was later abolished and the full cost of workmen's compensation put at the charge of the enterprise. Thus, the full circle was completed and the whole system came back to the notion of employers' liability for accidents.[6]

The common denominator behind all the different functions assigned to social security by the communist regime is the evident abuse of the institution for political purposes. However, this becomes in the end a double-edged weapon, which makes a significant contribution to the final downfall of the regime. Historically, the system develops in several stages. At the beginning, there is a legislative action in favour of social protection of the weak and disadvantaged classes of the population. Later comes the concept of reward for services, which tends to create privileged groups of regime supporters in the population. Then, over the years, the notion of weak and disadvantaged people will change sides, as these epithets will suitably designate chiefly the opponents of the regime and the persecuted groups. Between these two extremes is situated the vast majority of people, who are neither privileged nor persecuted, and who consider their political passivity a price to be paid for the 'social comfort' provided by the regime. However, in this particular setting, the regime has no room left for any reduction or retreat in social benefits policy on account of adverse economic circumstances.[7] Since continuing advance in social spending is the only choice, the resulting '*fuite en avant*' must sooner or later lead to the downfall of the whole system.

Many people think that communism as an important world ideology is dead and that it no longer constitutes a danger to a democratic society. Nothing could be further from the truth. It is particularly in the field of social security that its doctrine is dangerous since it concerns some of the most vulnerable aspects of the capitalist market economy. As we have already pointed out, it is a mistake to believe that in the closing years of the 1980s the communist world collapsed as result of an overall superiority of the capitalist system. Its implosion was due to a number of internal inconsistencies, above all that between its social ambitions and the effectiveness of its system of production. But the real debate regarding the value of its social innovations as compared with social policies of Western democracies has never taken place. Those ready to listen carefully to what some refer to as 'nostalgic reminiscences' echoed nowadays among the population in Eastern Germany will immediately recognise the source. It is a safe bet that with the increasing economic difficulties of the capitalist world, communism or some of its ideological varieties will soon start again recovering political ground among the hard-pressed populations. The danger will last as long as the capitalist system remains incapable of finding solutions to problems such as the political control of the world economy, mass unemployment and an effective integration of social and economic policies.

## Social security and neoliberalism

Classical economic theories were never at ease with the concept of social security. The principle of social solidarity underlying its whole philosophy cannot be accommodated within a doctrine based on the pursuit of self-interest and the maximisation of profits. Attempts made in the past to overcome this difficulty have never been successful, the reason being the basic and omnipresent duality of an individual's existence in society, once as an economic actor of production and consumption, once as the ultimate object and raison d'être of all efforts developed in a democratic society.

A study of the history of the liberal doctrine in relation to questions of social welfare will not throw much light on present neoliberal attitudes. If we look at the situation in Britain at the beginning of the 20th century, we will note that the New Liberals contributed greatly to the foundation of the welfare state by insisting on the introduction of social insurance as one of the means of raising 'the left-out millions' above a line below which the state should not let them fall (Churchill, 1909), and had some difficulties in distinguishing themselves clearly from certain policies of the upcoming Labour Party. At that time, they led an attack against the capitalist economy of the 19th century and against 'the establishment', which had tolerated its inhumanity (Marshall, 1965, p 47).

The neoliberalism as we know it today takes its roots in the belief in the supremacy of market forces as a guiding principle of societal development and in the refusal of any unorthodox intervention into the laws of the economy. The creation of wealth being the result of a free play of market forces, any redistribution of income is an unwelcome interference with these processes. The neoliberal ideological current has always been present in Western society even during the years of the biggest expansion of the welfare state, but it has never succeeded in attracting sufficient attention in a world bent on post-war reconstruction, creating institutional instruments of social justice and producing new forms of international collaboration. It is only in the aftermath of the first oil shocks in the early 1970s that the Chicago school of economists animated by students of Friedrich von Hayek began to be listened to. This was taking place in the midst of repeated economic crises when many people were looking for a potential culprit responsible for the deterioration of economic conditions. The expansion of the neoliberal doctrine was greatly facilitated by the extraordinary capacity of the Chicago school and its supporters relentlessly to push forward their ideas through an international network of institutions and research centres, using a very persuasive approach in spreading the new dogma. The neoliberals not only propose a specific economic theory, they also preach a new moral and social philosophy in fairly self-contained packing.

Presented as the new free world ideology, the movement first conquered and occupied the position of power in the world financial institutions, which gained an extraordinary importance in the light of given economic circumstances. Turning their attention to the problems of the developing world, its supporters elaborated, in the late 1980s, the so-called 'Washington consensus', as a result of which classical structures of social insurance in Latin America, instead of being reformed, were replaced by private arrangements used in the model pension scheme of Chile.[8] At about the same time, communist rule in Central and Eastern Europe collapsed and some of the new leaders found it only too easy to replace one political dogma with another; their decision to join the club ensured at the same time an access to international financing of certain reforms. From there on, it was possible to start invading Western European states whose governments found political support for the new credo. Fortunately, some powerful critics raised their voice when the mistaken turn of the World Bank's policy became evident – at an early stage we find among them Mesa-Lago (1996) followed by Orszak and Stiglitz (1999) and Barr (2000) – and this criticism led eventually to a partial change in the stand of the World Bank. But the harm was done and certain political forces were put into motion to continue a slow but steady demolition of the welfare state.

Admittedly, the worldwide crash of financial markets in the early years of the 2000s, exposing beyond any doubt the irrationality of the belief that they may constitute a superior form of social security provision for the individual, marked a pause in the dynamic expansion of the neoliberal doctrine. But it is astonishing to note that this demonstration of the fallacy of the neoliberal approach to social welfare did not spell the end of the whole enterprise. No doubt, by that time, the experience in several countries was that under certain political circumstances, and faced with the threat of continuing mass unemployment, you can get away with some measures aimed at the retrenchment of the welfare state without losing the next election. This may have provoked some political circles, which are not necessarily staunch supporters of the new ideology, to follow the trend and see what may come out of it. Unfortunately, the confusion regarding the basic principles of social welfare created in people's mind by the Chicago school reached a point where many politicians, not to mention members of the general public, practically lost the sense of orientation. The financial crisis of 2008 confirms this point.

In view of the importance (for the whole of this process and subsequent developments) of the World Bank (1994) report on old-age pensions, it is worthwhile examining it in more detail. Produced by a team of experts, the report constitutes an all-round attack on classical schemes of old-age insurance normally financed by a system of bi- or tripartite contributions on a pay-as-you-go basis. It suggests to governments to replace it with a three-pillar system, as follows:

(1) a publicly managed, tax-financed system with mandatory participation, providing a means-tested, flat-rate or minimum guaranteed pension;
(2) a privately managed, regulated and fully funded mandatory savings system, providing access to personal or occupational savings plans;
(3) voluntary fully funded personal or occupational savings plans.

The rationale of the proposal is spelled out in the introduction to the report:

> By separating the redistributive function from the savings function, the public pillar – and the size of the payroll tax needed to support it – can be kept relatively small, thus avoiding many of the growth-inhibiting problems associated with a dominant public pillar. (World Bank, 1994, p xiv)

The intention is to keep the benefit at the minimum level with the 'limited goal of reducing poverty among the old'.

The report is primarily aimed at developing countries, which constitute the principal field of intervention of the World Bank and whose experience is reflected in its pages. However, this does not prevent the message from being sent also to countries of the Organisation for Economic Co-operation and Development (OECD), whose pension schemes are supposed to have perverse effects by redistributing from the poor to the rich and are expected to produce intergeneration conflicts. Moreover, these pension schemes 'discourage work, saving and productive capital formation – thus contributing to economic stagnation' (World Bank, 1994, p 4).

Although the text speaks vaguely about 'spreading the insurance function across all three pillars' (p xiv), the proposal makes it plain that its only authorised institutional form is private insurance. Social insurance thus disappears from the world of old-age protection systems although it is a morally superior technique of social protection, based as it is on the idea of solidarity within a defined population group, which finds expression in the act of the pooling of resources and granting benefits as of right. It also completely disappears as an instrument of income redistribution. According to the authors, in a system of redistribution, shifting of income across groups creates injustice and hinders economic growth; on the other hand, 'making benefits directly contingent on contributions according to market principles discourages evasion, labour disincentive effects and political pressure leading to inefficient and inequitable outcomes' (1994, p 76).[9]

The new model of social welfare is couched in new terminology. 'Savings' is the key word, which dominates the operation of the model. The term 'social insurance contribution' is replaced by 'pay-roll tax'. But the masterpiece of the World Bank's report is the worldwide launch of the terminology referring to 'defined benefits' and 'defined contributions' schemes. One of the greatest achievements of classical social insurance expressing the very essence of social security has been the assurance of a given level of income in old age. Taking away this guarantee and opening the door to 'undefined benefits' amounts to an action aimed at the liquidation of social security as a social institution. The technical form of the attack is faultless: to the would-be expert audience, 'defined contribution scheme' sounds much more serious than a simple savings plan. Nevertheless, the fact that a social insecurity option is being proposed to governments by an international authority represents a major departure from the existing practice.

In professional international circles, the report, which was obviously meant to be provocative, was perceived as such. In a relatively short time, a major opposition was drummed up to contest the whole World

Bank approach to this subject. If some elements of the plan could meet certain problems found in developing countries, it was hardly applicable to the rest of the world; for the industrialised countries of Western Europe, the adoption of the plan as a whole was politically simply not conceivable. While remaining within the limits of established relations between organisations of the United Nations family, the International Labour Office developed in due time its own reply to the pension challenge raised by the World Bank (Gillion, 2000).

It starts with the premise that the objective of the pension reform is to ensure simultaneously full coverage with good governance, so as to prevent poverty in old age and provide indexed, guaranteed and reliable pensions for those on average incomes. One of the fundamental principles of social security pensions is that the retirement income of workers should be predictable and guaranteed and this cannot be achieved by defined contribution schemes. However, as it seems necessary to avoid conflict between normative principles and the wish to develop more direct links between contribution and benefits, the first ILO design consists of financing retirement incomes from a range of different sources, in particular a mixture of defined benefit and defined contribution schemes, such as shown in the following schema:

(1) a bottom anti-poverty tier, means-tested and financed from general revenues, which would provide income support for those without other means;
(2) a second, pay-as-you-go defined benefit tier, mandatory and publicly managed, which would provide a moderate but fully indexed replacement rate for all those who had contributed to it;
(3) a defined contribution tier, mandatory up to a determined ceiling and possibly privately managed, which would provide pension annuities;
(4) a voluntary and privately managed defined contribution tier without any ceiling.

Such a structure would permit splitting the risks inherent in pension schemes – both political risks associated with the public management of defined benefit schemes and the market risks associated with defined contribution schemes – but would at the same time provide a basic, guaranteed retirement income for the large majority of workers with average income. However, the final conclusion is that:

> There is no single design which fits all countries and all circumstances. The question of what is the most appropriate

> design has to be weighed against the other factors, in
> particular the historical and social context and the need to
> provide universal coverage and good governance. (Gillion,
> 2000, p 63)

This would seem to put an appropriate end to the World Bank
incursion into the field of social security, which only leaves behind
its particular terminology, hiding in technical terms the postulate,
now generally admitted, of reducing social expenditure on pensions
to a level supportable by the present state of the global economy. But
it is far from being the end of the impact of neoliberal ideology on
developments in this sector.

A very typical example of this impact is shown by the treatment of
social protection issues in the accession process, which led, early in 2004,
to the affiliation of a number of countries of the post-communist world
to the EU. Admittedly, this was not an easy exercise given the fact the
EU itself was – as it is up to the present – unsure about finding its way to
a necessary equilibrium between social and economic policy. The social
policy sector being subject to decision making by national authorities of
each member state, and the inbuilt asymmetry of the attention given to
social policy as compared with economic matters, gave the impression
of a great confusion in the whole process. Thus, it was not unusual
to find in the same national accession report a great deal of praise
and even congratulations to the respective government for the results
obtained in the field of social security reforms, while pronouncing
the most serious warning against uncontrolled expenditure of the
institutions concerned in chapters dealing with public finance. In fact,
in spite of the rhetoric about social cohesion current at that time in
official circles, the EU accession procedures were mainly interested in
the financial aspects of social security institutions and their impact on
public expenditure. Most of the proposals formulated in these reports
aimed at lowering the level of social security expenditure for the sake
of the consolidation of the state budget and at the restructuring of the
whole social system. This bias was so blatant that it prompted some
experts to speak about a 'hidden agenda' of EU proposals, unmistakably
following the neoliberal approach of economic advisors of the World
Bank (Ferge, 2000).

Other developments highlighting the impact of the neoliberal attack
on social security could be observed in the field of occupational
pensions. The first example comes from Switzerland where, as a result
of the collapse of financial markets during the years 2001 and 2002, the
mandatory occupational pension funds found themselves for the first

time in history below the legally prescribed level of capital reserves. The government hence intervened and requested the funds to lower from 4% to 2% the minimum annual rate of interest on individual accounts as well as the conversion rate of capital into pension, this move resulting in an average 20% reduction in the level of pensions served under the scheme. When two years later, in 2005, the investment returns were back to 11%, and the government refused to change the prescribed rates on the ground of the need to take account of a five-year average performance, some national newspapers spoke about 'a hold-up of the century'.[10] Manifestly, the short-term economic considerations inspired by the neoliberal way of thinking clashed with the long-term preoccupation regarding the solvency of funds – and such clashes are likely to accompany all future negotiations.

A more dramatic change could be observed in the development of the occupational pensions in Britain. According to surveys conducted in the course of 2004, the country was witnessing the end of defined benefit schemes in large companies of the private sector. One after another, the companies were closing their final-salary schemes to new members, replacing them with the new and fashionable defined contribution schemes, or – taking advantage of the legislation on stakeholder pensions of 2001 facilitating some coverage for employees in firms with no pension arrangements – with nothing at all. Investigation into the causes of this unusually rapid development revealed that this was not simply a question of business considerations but rather a question of what has been referred to as 'herd behaviour' of employers in the context of a changing social environment (Bridgen and Meyer, 2005). But it seems reasonable to suggest that to start the movement, some very powerful factors had to be at play in a country with a very long tradition of occupational pensions. One of them was no doubt the official blessing given to employers who had decided to abandon any pretension of providing old-age security for their employees by the neoliberal reformers.

By granting respectability to any action aimed at dismantling the welfare state, neoliberalism, under the leadership of the World Bank, has potentially cleared the way for a relatively rapid transition to a world without social security. In an earlier version of the manuscript of this chapter, the closing sentence read: 'The question is, how long is it likely to last before further experience with neoliberal reforms reveals their fallacy?' The reader may wish to refer to the closing chapter of this book and more particularly to the section entitled 'The initial impact of the present economic crisis' to find the answer.

## Social security and solidarity

The concept of social solidarity is among the most ancient themes of political philosophy. In modern dictionaries, 'solidarity' usually refers to a relationship between persons who are conscious of a community of interest between them. Some refer to several meanings of solidarity and distinguish between the awareness of belonging to a group, and the feeling of moral obligation towards other members of a group. Popular usage today would no doubt include this last element in the definition.

Historically, different perceptions of solidarity have tended to reflect different cultural traditions and political convictions of their authors. In France, towards the close of the 19th century, a few years after Emile Durkheim had published his analysis differentiating between mechanical and organic solidarity (*De la division du travail social*, 1893), Léon Bourgeois formulated a new doctrine inspired by the philosophy of solidarity (*Solidarité*, 1896) to provide an ideological reply of the French radical party to the expanding revolutionary socialism (Mièvre, 2005). In an attempt to reach a synthesis between the ideas of individualistic liberalism and collectivist socialism, he sought to put an end to class struggle by achieving 'not socialisation of property, but socialisation of individuals' (p 7). His concept of solidarity was based on the recognition of the social duty that every human being has towards society; since an individual cannot live alone without society, they must pay their debt for all they receive from it. And it is on this notion that he built the concept of solidarity in the sense of mutual help among all members of society, implying a duty towards those who suffer. While education plays the central role in the process of socialisation of individuals, the state must also assume a role in facilitating the development of a system of insurance against 'natural incapacities' such as childhood, disability or old age, and mutual insurance against social risks such as accidents or unemployment.[11]

The notion of solidarity is naturally present in the main institutional predecessors of social insurance, that is, mutual aid and public assistance, the extent depending on the definition of the human collective at the base. However, not all of these institutional channels practise the same degree of solidarity with the same consequences. It seems obvious that mutual aid is closer to the notion of solidarity among members of the same group than public assistance, originally associated with a protective action of society against its unworthy members and only much later with a notion of public help to those in need. The discretionary nature of social assistance contradicts most openly the principle of equality among those who give and those who receive and automatically associates this type of solidarity with charity. As we have pointed out before, the moral value of solidarity expressed through social insurance is incomparably higher than that of public assistance, due to a special regard for the principle of equality and human dignity safeguarded by virtue of benefits granted as of right.

Political preferences regarding the concept of solidarity will largely depend on the attitude towards the state. An ideology favouring a strong state intervention in favour of weaker members of society will not hesitate to impose an institutional expression of solidarity on all citizens, while that opposing excessive powers of the state will prefer to give them free choice, with the risk of failing to achieve the desired objective. During the early years of the 20th century, liberal circles in most countries were opposed to the introduction of social insurance mainly because of the obligatory nature of the institution, estimating that it was contrary to the principle of the free choice of the individual in providing for their protection. In our time, the supporters of neoliberal ideology tend to express their preference for solidarity through social assistance for reasons of economic efficiency, social insurance being accused of wasting financial resources through the indiscriminate shedding of social benefits over selected population groups including individuals who may not need them. Needless to say, the discretionary character of the 'assistancial' type of solidarity makes it also less expensive for the public purse and the taxpayer.

We may also examine in this context the solidarity aspect of social assistance as a public service. If the grant of a benefit to a weaker member of society is based on the same principle as, for instance, the supply of water or energy, the act of solidarity is reduced to the observance of civic discipline regarding the payment of taxes. It becomes part of a general concept of solidarity underlying the very existence of human society, close to the mechanical solidarity of Durkheim's theory. However, this is not the kind of solidarity needed to secure the required degree of social cohesion in a modern society. The latter demands, in addition to an active feeling of belonging to the body of citizens, a feeling of moral obligation towards its weaker members, embodied in the concept of social security.

A complete analysis of different aspects of solidarity cannot leave aside the school of thought that puts an equals sign between social solidarity and individual interest. Ever since the beginning of human history it has been recognised that it is plainly in the interest of each individual to conform to the behaviour dictated by the group solidarity. Some go even further so as to suggest that if we remain at the level of rational choices, all motivations of human behaviour might be reduced to the question of self-interest (Coleman, 1990). Without going any deeper into these considerations, it may be useful, nevertheless, to have a look at their practical implications from the point of view of future social security policy.

As far as the institution of social insurance is concerned, the presence of self-interest among its basic motivations is fairly obvious. It is taken for granted for members of low-income classes, it is evident for members of the middle-income classes and it may be less evident but still holds true for some members of the upper-income classes. Nobody would deny that even a rich man may fall victim to an accident, which will prevent him from earning his living. Should this require very expensive medical treatment and long-term care, he may not be rich enough to be able to afford it. The question is hence how rich do you have to be to become risk-free without social security?

If we are able to demonstrate that in the social insurance concept the spectrum of solidarity is legitimately stretching from the moral obligation to help weaker members of society to the pursuit of self-interest, the public argument in favour of the institution should tend to underline the self-interest aspect so as to obtain adhesion of a larger number of citizens. The volume of popular support would then be likely to depend on the degree of transparency in the relationship between the social insurance contribution and the potential benefit. This could mark an important step on the way towards the rationalisation of the whole social protection system while avoiding an unhealthy situation observed by some authors in the past when the lack of transparency may have served the adoption of certain social policies (Baldwin, 1990).

In the same way, an effort should be made to dissociate the term 'solidarity' from its current political connotation. It is especially in the French-speaking countries that *solidarité* is still being used to describe a social protection system with a high level of income redistribution between different classes of the population. Given the present political climate and the evolution of the world economy, this insistence no longer serves the interests of lower-income groups who are threatened with a progressive dismantlement of existing social protection systems. A more appropriate strategy would be to render the institution its original purpose and seek the widest possible political consensus so as to ensure the continuity of its operations.

## Social security and democracy

There is a close link between social security and political systems in all countries – as we shall demonstrate in Part Two of this book, the institution is directly dependent on the working of the political forces in society. The introduction of social insurance in Bismarck's Germany was a political act with a precise political purpose. In any democratic country, social security is an indispensable part of the political programme of the government and the adoption of a corresponding legislation requires a good deal of political consensus among political parties.

One of the main functions of social security is to protect the individual from the loss of social status and from a sudden deterioration of material conditions necessary for the exercise of his personal freedom. To show the way to 'freedom from want' was the chief objective of the Beveridge Report (1942), which marked the collective memory of generations. To the extent that only free people are capable of building democratic societies, social protection institutions ensure the necessary preconditions for the establishment and maintenance of a democratic system of government. It seems obvious that people need to have a shelter and be free from hunger and incapacitating disease in order to be able to turn their minds to questions regarding the quality of the society they wish to live in.

Another supporting pillar of a democratic society that finds its expression in social security is the principle of social justice. Every move towards better social justice inevitably contributes to the internal cohesion of society and to the elimination of social conflicts. This impact is felt beyond the frontiers of national societies and has a bearing on the international situation and on conflicts among nations. This is exactly what was present in the minds of the delegates at the 1944 Philadelphia conference of the ILO when, at the close of a long and horrible war, they adopted their motto: 'No lasting peace without social justice'. And only a few years later, those who succeeded in reconstructing its daughter organisation ISSA lost no time in adding a second line: 'No social justice without social security'.

Depending on the institutional form it may take, social security also tends to reinforce democracy on account of the positive impact of its everyday operations on civil society. In a classical social insurance scheme, particularly in countries such as France or Germany, the running of the institution is largely in the hands of social partners in cooperation with other organisations of civil society. This represents a real school of democracy through participative management, under the overall supervision of the state. Activities of various social services, which often accompany the operations of different branches of social security, provide an excellent example of the involvement of civil society in the pursuit of nationwide social protection objectives.

We may hence agree that social security is good for democracy. But what if we reverse the question and ask whether democracy is good for social security? The reply is far from straightforward and calls for a careful examination of different national situations. It inevitably implies a value judgement regarding different types of society, different settings in which the institution operates and the intrinsic value of the institution itself.

The first reflection concerns the relationship between the political system in a country and its social security system. Our previous discussion of social security under communism indicates that a certain type of social security, with a highly important redistributive function, can be set up in non-democratic systems. In fact, history shows that a totalitarian type of society can build its social security scheme more rapidly precisely because it is non-democratic and does not have to go through the process of a lengthy and careful weighting of interests of political parties or population groups. Moreover, the result of an evaluation based on a purely economic analysis may be plainly in favour of non-democratic countries, as shown by a recent study where three US economists found that 'democracies spend a little less of their GDP on social security, grow their budgets a bit more slowly, and cap their payroll tax more often, than do economically and demographically similar nondemocracies' (Mulligan et al, 2002, p 1). This leaves us with the question of what determines the different quality of social security schemes established by democratic and non-democratic societies.

The experience of the communist abuse of the institution suggests that for the evaluation of social security measures within a society it is not enough to examine the situation from the point of view of the material security of individual existence; it is also necessary to take into account the quality of this existence in the respective societal environment. Social security is hence not only an income maintenance technique for certain contingencies, that is, a defensive measure ensuring protection against social risks, but also, and above all, an offensive measure ensuring freedom of full participation in social life. This means that the Beveridge postulate of freedom from want also has a positive counterpart in freedom *for* realising the objectives of a democratic society. A social institution so close to the moral image of the society it serves cannot be judged independently from its declared objectives and social values.

Having established that, the question still remains whether, in practice, the institution is being used in an appropriate way in our democracies? Can the politicians resist the temptation to use this important policy instrument for the sake of staying in power? The real dilemma that social security creates for a democratic society concerns the tendency that political parties will always have to attract the popular vote by proposing social benefits that may not be justified in the light of the existing social conditions or which may overstrain the financial resources. The most efficient way of controlling this situation would be a full transparency of the financial flows involved in social security operations, and – more fundamentally perhaps – a better education of the population so as to make it easier for them to recognise what is in their medium- and long-term interests. It goes without saying that more and better knowledge of the working of the institution would also be the best way towards arriving at a higher degree of general consensus on the level of social spending in a democratic society.

## Notes

[1] This would not apply to managers of several industrial enterprises in France who in the spring of 2009 became the object of sequestration by workers threatened by unemployment, nor to the directors of the firm New Fabris in Chatellerault (France) who in July 2009 had to face the menace of the factory being blown up by desperate employees requesting a correct end-of-work compensation.

[2] Thus, for instance, in the everyday practice of the International Social Security Association (ISSA) in Geneva, social security was what ISSA member organisations in different countries considered it to be.

[3] This point was well recognised by most of the communist regimes in post-war Europe, which pompously scrapped social insurance contributions in their state systems, declaring them superior to those in the capitalist countries precisely because working people did not have to pay.

[4] This issue represents one of the key concepts of Marx's analysis of class struggle where it leads to the notion of the alienation of labour. Recognising the economic theory of *commodification of labour* as being a 'central concern of modern philosophy, ideology and social theory', Esping-Andersen (1990, pp 35-54) deals at some length with the question of 'decommodification in social policy'.

[5] The first category, where pensions could be drawn after 15 years of work, was reserved for miners, aviators, seamen and metal workers; the second category covered employees exposed to infectious diseases, radioactive materials or toxic substances; and the third category embraced all remaining employees representing some 90% of the total workforce. Some authors suggest that the

creation of categories of employment was not a question of a deliberate policy but rather that of an administrative incapacity to cover from the beginning the whole working population.

[6] In Bulgaria, the regime went even further and reduced the salaries of foremen in factory departments where accidents occurred.

[7] This was the experience of the Czechoslovak government after the reform of 1964, which introduced, among others, the principle of imposition of pensions and stopped the practice of cumulating pension and salary. This reform may have been among the causes of the reformist movement in subsequent years, leading eventually to the 'Prague Spring'.

[8] It should be recalled that the World Bank pension plan for developing countries was strongly influenced by the 'structural reform' of the pension system implemented in 1980-81 in Chile, which replaced its public pension schemes by a private pension system. For details of this and of the subsequent evolution of pension schemes in Latin America, see Mesa-Lago (2008).

[9] This statement is interesting in so far as it favours 'benefits directly contingent on contributions'. So why not social insurance, which is based on the same principle? No doubt, because social insurance operations are motivated by other than 'market principles'.

[10] For the full text, see an article entitled 'Deuxième pilier: immunité pour le casse du siècle', *Tribune de Genève*, 5 May 2006, p 11.

[11] It will be noted that Léon Bourgeois played a prominent role in the adoption of the first French law on workers' and peasants' pensions in 1910.

---

# THREE

# The new approaches to securing human existence in society

In the first chapter of this book we briefly recalled the history of social security from the time of its institutional predecessors to its conceptual reorganisation and expansion in the post-war years and the beginning of its retrenchment in more recent decades. In this chapter we will review in more detail the changes that have taken place in our societal environment, leading to the situation of growing social insecurity throughout the globalised world and to the present economic crisis, the impact of which on the institution is still difficult to measure.

## The road to social insecurity

Among the most important changes that have taken place in advanced societies enjoying a reasonable degree of social protection has been a relatively rapid and profound modification of their age structure. Spectacular improvements have been achieved in longevity – life expectancy at birth, which was about 66 years in the middle of 20th century, is currently 80 years – while there has been an overall decline in fertility. As a result, the ageing society is unable to maintain old-age provisions as c onceived during the post-war years and cannot provide security in old age through public provisions only. These have to be reduced to an economically acceptable level and completed by other measures requiring diversification of resources. Whatever the resulting mix, it seems obvious that the individual capacity to save and contribute rather than an objectively defined need will determine the level of old-age benefits in future.

Profound mutations have also occurred in the economic life of global society. While democratic countries based on capitalist market economy experienced growing difficulties, triggered by abrupt changes in the supply and price of oil, the ruling regimes in planned economy countries, failing to adapt to social and economic evolution, lost the remaining political support of their populations and collapsed in the middle of serious upheavals. At the same time, helped by the revolution in communication technology and carried by a human rights vision of neoliberal ideology, a rapid globalisation process was set into motion, spelling the end of former prosperity of the Western world. As a result of that, the reduced economic growth was no longer sufficient to finance what has been known as 'acquired rights' and benefits of the post-war welfare state. For some time, institutional structures of social security, deeply embedded in the living tissue of society, continued to perform their functions, showing a remarkable resilience to the pressure of adverse factors. However, at the end of the 20th century a general trend towards the retrenchment of the welfare state began to dominate the international scene.

Admittedly, not all share this view, and some would argue that throughout the past decades of the so-called crisis, the welfare state was in fact rolling on. Having cushioned a soft landing in most advanced countries after a series of economic difficulties in the 1970s and 1980s, it was affected by the globalisation trend and by demographic ageing. However, according to some authors basing their judgement on current analyses of welfare expenditure (Castles, 2004), the anticipation of the growing pressure on public spending has been grossly exaggerated and the predicted doom of the welfare state has not taken place. In their view, many countries appear to have the necessary capacity to maintain steady welfare expenditure and are likely to continue to do so for some time to come.

Nevertheless, any grassroots observer of the situation in the Western industrialised world will note that there has been a clear deterioration in social welfare benefits especially with regard to main social protection sectors such as old age and health. The pension field is particularly affected by the combined economic and demographic pressure and the signs of deterioration are clearly visible. There has been a gradual reduction in the size of the public pensions sector – this becoming a basic residual pillar rarely aiming at more than the maintenance of a minimum standard of living – and a simultaneous increase in the importance of the occupational sector. However, the latter is also subject to considerable pressures, be it on account of a general move away from the concept of defined benefits to that of defined contributions, or be it on account of fluctuating financial markets.

In the health protection sector, the stage is being set to cover the necessary minimum, leaving it to the individual to assume responsibility, according to their means, for small healthcare expenditure on one side and for more than standard care on the other. More than any other branch of social security, healthcare is essentially a question of cultural standards, and considerable variations exist between different countries. In Western countries, a great resistance is shown to what some call the emergence of two societies in a sector, which people instinctively feel should be governed by the principle of equal treatment. Nevertheless, in a capitalist market economy, the increasing cost of medical technology, and the natural desire of every individual to preserve the most precious possession in their life, can hardly lead to anything else. A similar divide is noticeable in former communist countries, accustomed to an open access to healthcare, where under the impact of new ideology many people refuse even the idea of social insurance, in favour of a hypothetical individual responsibility for one's own health.

While it is too early to estimate the full impact on the institution of the two successive waves of financial and economic instability that have occurred in the present decade, it seems obvious that the institutional model of social security established as a result of a long historical development no longer fits the present-day requirements and that a complete reappraisal of existing policies has to take place. Before advancing to further analysis, it would seem important to review the trends in social security developments that have emerged in most recent years as a reaction to the progressive change of the societal environment.

## Towards new approaches in industrialised countries

If we turn our attention to Europe, we will not discover any new mechanism invented to deal with the present situation, but rather a series of shifts in emphasis on different elements in the existing structures and different roles assigned to specific actors. Thus, the state, while reducing its direct involvement in running social security schemes and providing social welfare benefits, is at the same time greatly increasing its powers when it comes to regulating occupational or private arrangements. Simultaneously, and this constitutes no doubt a historical regression, there is an obvious shift of responsibility back to employers and different forms of occupational welfare, back to families and their supporting role, and also back to the individual and their personal capacity to save for rainy days.

The lesson that has been learned in recent decades, marked by mass unemployment, is the importance of work for the preservation or further development of social security systems. 'Getting people on benefit back to work as soon as possible is the number one priority of most European countries in the early years of the new century. It is apparent in all areas of social protection' (Kessler, 2005, p 67). In the field of unemployment benefits, the new elements in the prevailing formula are the reinforcement of the obligation to accept work, active search of employment and training. This is a logical trend, as a result of which the grant of a benefit tends to represent only a residual measure in comparison with investments required for other provisions seeking to improve the beneficiary's employability. However, as mentioned earlier in this book, there is a danger involved in this new approach of a possible 'instrumentalisation' of social security in relation to other public policy goals; it may lead to a confusion regarding the ultimate objectives respectively of employment promotion and of social security. While the former is a value-neutral instrument of economic policy, the latter belongs to the realm of the categorical imperative of social justice. It would be a very bad service to render to humankind if social security came to be regarded primarily as an instrument of employment policy.

Another noticeable trend concerns an increasing mix in the sources of finance of social security measures as a result of a frequent resort to taxation. This was apparent from the very beginning of the economic slowdown, the politicians seeking to complete insufficient funds raised from contributions by ad hoc levies within the general taxation system. To have recourse to earmarked social security taxes has the advantage of not overloading the contributory system while enjoying better reception on the part of the taxpayer as compared with other levies. However, as argued earlier, this kind of emergency financing, which consists of mixing institutional principles and finalities, initiates a process that tends to transform social security policy into a political expedient.

At the same time, there is an increasing trend to use tax measures as an instrument of social policy. Admittedly, different types of 'tax credits' have always been part of the government panoply of measures used to alleviate the situation of particular population groups or income classes. But in more recent years, these measures, widely used in European countries such as the UK, France and Germany, seem to indicate the presence of a new approach to dealing with individual needs. Under the cover of relatively small institutional reforms, they follow a different logic of welfare likely to lead to a major systemic change (Palier, 2008).

This development calls for extreme caution since it reflects a very short-term and purely economic approach to welfare measures. The gradual switch in the field of social security from social insurance to social assistance techniques is taking place in line with neoliberal ideology, opposing income transfers between different groups of the population but recognising that those who cannot cope with the requirements of a free competitive society have to receive some economic help from the state. Whatever legal arrangements may govern such mixed schemes, it seems obvious that they will lose the character of providing benefits as of right and turn them into discretionary measures, carrying a stigma. This will have a negative impact on the spirit of self-reliance, which is of fundamental importance for social development and will undermine the establishment of democratic ways of living expected to govern relations among people of equal standing.

It would hence seem important to use the opportunity of the present economic upheaval, which is calling for a drastic reform of the institution, for a fundamental rethinking of social security policy in line with the hard facts of current developments. Political acceptability based on a large consensus, economic sustainability adapted to the performance of existing national economies and redistributive transparency of transfers operated by social insurance schemes should be the key words of this effort.

## Social security and the developing world

Social security started expanding in the developing world in the middle of the 20th century. Due to specific circumstances, only Latin America had an early start, in some cases before or during the Second World War, other continents following later, mostly after the nations concerned gained independence from former colonial powers. Some social protection institutions had already been created during the colonial period, such as provident funds in the English-speaking countries of Africa and Asia, basically representing only obligatory savings for old age. The initial social protection measure found in the countries under the French colonial administration usually took the form of family allowance funds. Understandably, these institutions as well as all other classical social insurance schemes could be established only for that part of the population living in a structured economic sector providing employment – hence the paradox of building social protection for people who under the circumstances occupied a privileged position in their society. But there was no conceivable alternative at that time. The choice to go ahead with social security schemes for people in regular employment was fully justified as a measure that helped to preserve and reinforce the newly formed labour force, representing the driving power of future economic development. Given the general trend of economic progress, it was only a question of time before new and constantly expanding categories of the population could in turn be covered.

The deterioration of economic growth in the last decades of the 20th century brought this development to a halt and, in certain continents, together with a dramatic change in health conditions, transformed it into a regression spiral. With the prospect of future economic progress being less promising and with the worldwide movement against poverty and exclusion demanding more effective action, the strategy of social progress in developing countries is now being questioned and emphasis laid on the improvement of living conditions of people outside the labour market. Some do not hesitate to blame the Western egocentrism for focusing attention on measures aimed at maintaining the income of the worker, while in fact the priority preoccupation should have been the guarantee of a subsistence minimum for the main bulk of the population.

For several years now the ILO has been making efforts so as to attract to this problem the attention of the international public interested in questions of social policy. The authors of a recent article on the subject, referring to the preliminary results of the ongoing New ILO Social Security Inquiry, point out that:

> between 70 and 80% of the global population live in a state of more or less severe 'social insecurity', i.e. have no access to formal social security beyond the often limited possibilities of families, kinship groups or communities to secure their standard of living. (Cichon and Hagemejer, 2007, p 173)

They subsequently argue that to the extent that social security systems are a necessary part of the institutional framework of any effective market economy, the introduction of a basic social protection floor in developing countries would be both a desirable and an affordable investment in their social and economic development.

This substantive change of international social policy perspective calls for a more thorough analysis of the problem at hand. First of all, it needs to be said that the strategy for developing countries that consists of securing the newly formed labour force in regular employment is fundamentally sound whatever the circumstances. Should some measure of basic income redistribution among wider circles of the population be envisaged, this wealth has first to be created before it can be redistributed. Consequently, any change in social security strategy to help the impoverished masses outside the structured sector can only be contemplated as a step taken in addition to the classical income maintenance scheme and not in its place. In other words, it has to reinforce the social security system in the country rather than weaken its future development.[1] But it seems evident that, whatever the circumstances, this extra effort will require important means and resources to be drawn from available social funds at the expense of other schemes and their more rapid development. This fact will have to be squarely faced and no complacent attitude allowed obscuring the choice.

---

In searching for ways of improving the situation of the vast masses of the population outside the structured sector, care must be taken so as to avoid confusing objectives and techniques of social protection measures. It is particularly in relation to solving social security problems of the third world that the importance of clearly distinguishing between salary-based contributions leading to the grant of benefits as of right, and taxation-based discretionary social aid benefits becomes apparent. It seems obvious that the idea of covering total populations in developing countries for classical contingencies will belong for some time to come to the realm of utopia. But this does not mean that further attempts should not be made to make available to additional population groups benefits or services provided under the schemes for people in regular employment. The whole history of social security is the history of its progressive expansion on the way to universal coverage.

If, on the other hand, the intention is to launch from the start some kind of basic subsistence grant for the benefit of large population groups, the social insurance approach cannot be envisaged and other means have to be developed to try to meet the challenge. It may be assumed that the approach used in the case of many existing schemes for rural populations, which consists of identifying first what constitutes an income guarantee (e.g. crop, cattle and so on) may not operate when applied to a multifaceted problem of maintaining the livelihood of masses of people living outside regular economic structures. Given the excessive riches created by the capitalist economy in many parts of the world, it may not be unthinkable that some huge 'venture capital' is used to invest in a low economy starter country offering a guarantee of a basic subsistence minimum to the whole population. But even in such a case, the risks would be enormous in view of the – by necessity – temporary nature of the experiment and also of the moral hazard involved.

The general problem we have to face in developing countries is that of using social insurance schemes for combating endemic poverty. In the industrialised world, these schemes were intended essentially to prevent poverty likely to be provoked by a number of specified risks or circumstances. This is not the case in developing countries where poverty is the inherent condition of a majority of the population and where other means have to be used as a chief weapon against poverty. Nevertheless, the role of social security in these countries is equally important, if not more, because of its impact on the maintenance of those in regular employment. This amounts to the recognition of a potential conflict between social insurance and tax-benefit schemes. In fact, some relational problems have already been reported in recent studies dealing with this problem. One of them refers to a tension presently manifest in Brazil, where representatives of social security institutions fear that tax-financed benefits may undermine the will of the population concerned to pay social insurance contributions (Barrientos, 2007, p 114). This question is of considerable importance for social protection policy of any developing country. There is a well-known tendency on the part of the population to take unearned social benefits for granted and this could make any ulterior policy change and move towards a contributory social welfare system even more difficult. If an active participation and direct involvement of the population in social projects is to be the rule, the future of social security in developing countries may largely depend on a careful evaluation of these choices.

\* \* \* \* \*

The above summaries of emerging trends in social security development during the early years of the present century indicate that there is a growing gap in the situation of industrialised and developing countries. One possible exception may be Latin America where in the closing years of the previous century nine countries followed the World Bank plan of privatisation of pensions. At the end of 2008, the Argentine government decided to put the clock back and abolish the pension scheme based on individual capitalisation, launched in 1994, and absorb it into the public pay-as-you-go scheme (Mesa-Lago, 2009). This move is the result of the recent financial crisis, the private pension funds concerned having lost some 20% of the value of their assets. However, it should be kept in mind that for a number of reasons, the evolution of social security in Latin America (Mesa-Lago, 2008) presents a somewhat special case among the developing countries.

As for the trends that are characteristic of the situation in industrialised countries, they seem to indicate a series of non-systemic reactions to current difficulties, threatening a gradual disruption of the whole system. None of them points in the direction of a fundamental change needed in the light of the current economic situation. We shall come back to this problem in the last chapter of this book, after an incursion into the macro-sociology of social security particularly suited to examining the evolution of the institution against the background of its societal environment.

**Note**

[1] This point is well made by van Ginneken and McKinnon (2007, p 15), who estimated that 'whereas emergent tax-financed social security in developing countries holds the promise of making an impact on global poverty and vulnerability, the main challenge is to ensure that this contributes to the development of comprehensive social security systems'.

# Part Two

Understanding social security in
its societal environment: which
methodology?

# FOUR

# A brief history of the sociology of social security

It would be rather difficult to try to establish a date on which the first sociological study of social security was presented to the interested public. Even before the middle of the 20th century, people concerned with this institution were writing essays that could easily qualify for this label, although 'sociology' is not once mentioned in the text.

## The beginning of the art: the quest for understanding

The search for origins becomes incomparably easier if we insist on the term 'sociology of social security' appearing in the title of the study. In such case, the obvious forerunner would be the Fourteenth National Congress of Sociology in Mexico, held in November 1963, which was entirely devoted to this theme.[1] Clearly, not all papers presented to the congress could legitimately be considered as contributions to the sociology of social security, but whatever the scientific value of this event, it nevertheless bore witness to an interest in sociology as a new tool for the study of the institution, which, at that time, was among the chief preoccupations of many countries.

The congress also marked the beginning of the subsequent involvement in this field of ISSA,[2] reflecting the widely felt need for an expert analysis of the institution by social scientists, in addition to that of lawyers, actuaries and statisticians. Sociology was not the only discipline to appear on the scene – with the growing importance of social security schemes in the national economy, it was natural that economists, interested in the operations and the impact of the institution, began to enter this area of study. In reaction to the general call for taking a measure of the economic dimension of the institution, the relationship between social security and national economy became one of the central themes of the International Conference of Social Security Actuaries and Statisticians, held in 1966 in Paris.

In the same year, ISSA took the initiative to bring an item dealing with sociological studies of social security to the agenda of the VIth World Congress of Sociology held in Evian (France). In collaboration with the International Sociological Association (ISA), a Round Table

Meeting on the Sociology of Social Security was convened within the programme of the congress to review the state of research in different countries and to map the essential issues regarding the objectives and the strategy of research in this field. Both comparative studies and country-specific papers were presented to the meeting, attended by some 40 participants.[3] It was made clear during the discussions that an effort aimed at relating the operational results of a social security scheme to its declared objectives could hardly be rewarding in view of the internal incoherence of national schemes due to particular conditions of their growth under governments with different political orientations. This pointed to the need to examine each national scheme within its own societal environment and in a broad cultural context. It was essential to carry out such examination in a historical perspective, since the experience with the working of a scheme appeared to be an important determining factor in the institution's further development. Thus, from the start, the sociological research highlighted the importance of what was later generally understood under the concept of 'path dependency'.

Before closing its discussions, the meeting proposed to reconvene similar round tables on the occasion of future sociological congresses and invited ISSA to take the necessary steps so as to develop a programme of study of social security by the social sciences. This suggestion was immediately followed up with the establishment, in October 1966, of an ISSA Study Group on Research, with the task of monitoring and coordinating research activities in this area. It was this group that subsequently guided collaboration with international bodies and academic institutions interested in the sociology of social security. Within its own research programme, ISSA opened the door to a multidisciplinary approach to studies of social security, closely related to the needs of its member organisations.

The second Round Table Meeting on the Sociology of Social Security was held within the framework of the VIIth World Congress of Sociology in 1970 in Varna (Bulgaria). Since the general theme of the congress was social planning, the ISSA meeting was devoted to the question of planning in social security. Ten papers dealing with conceptual analysis as well as national monographs on specific sectors or aspects of social security were presented to this meeting (ISSA, 1971). A follow-up ISSA research meeting on this subject was held in 1972 in Brussels, but by the time of the publication of its papers (ISSA, 1973) the first oil crisis appeared on the horizon, spelling a rapid end to the extraordinary expansion of social security and leaving little scope for further development of advanced planning.

The Varna meeting was the last event organised by ISSA on the occasion of a sociological congress. The reasons were partly technical; ISSA owed to its constituents a well-prepared meeting with documents and interpretation and this could hardly be ensured within a very large and more loosely organised international gathering. Furthermore, in view of the earlier-mentioned new emphasis on multidisciplinary research within ISSA, there was less opportunity to deal specifically with sociological studies. And finally, and perhaps more importantly, an evolution took place within ISA, in so far that one of its research groups, previously concerned mainly with poverty and social work, began gradually to cover the whole field of social security. In this way, the Research Committee on Poverty, Welfare and Social Policy (RC19), created in 1970, became the main international platform for sociological studies of social security.

The sudden upsurge of interest in the sociology of social security in the mid-1960s calls for some comments and explanations. It should be borne in mind that this was at the height of the period that witnessed a great expansion of the welfare state. The economic situation was flourishing and everybody believed that a significant annual growth of national income would continue to be a permanent feature of social development. In the field of social security, the emphasis was on the improvement of benefits and the coverage of new needs rather than on any limitation of social expenditure. The early studies were hence motivated by questions such as: why is social security developing so rapidly, how does the institution function and why is it different from one country to another? This quest for understanding was soon followed by the wish to apply the new knowledge to decision making in the field of planning and general orientation of the institution. Reflecting an obvious societal need, this interest was widely shared in international as well as national government and academic circles.[4] To the extent that in this period no major difficulties stood in the way of obtaining the necessary research funds, the conditions were set for a rapid start.

However, over the next few years, primary attention was given to sectoral studies of different aspects of social security, rather than to macro-sociological studies of the institution, a subject that 'had entirely ceased to be the concern of sociologists' (Sigg, 1986, p 285). In their approach, the researchers preferred either to consider social security as part of a broader range of questions within the framework of the sociology of social policy or of the welfare state (see Townsend, 1975; Room, 1979), or to give priority to a sectoral approach and study, from the sociological viewpoint, of only certain fields of social security. In his earlier-mentioned analysis, Sigg (1986) considered it extremely astonishing that in a period when social institutions, such as education, religion, the family and even leisure, were the subject of intense sociological research, a highly important component of the institutional network – social security – was left aside. His suggestion that perhaps sociology had no clear perception of the role of this institution needs some elaboration.

Part of the explanation may lie in the fact that social security is an extremely complex institution. The correct understanding of its functions, which is essential for any sociological research, requires a fair amount of work; this in itself may have served as a deterrent to those not wishing to get involved in a long preliminary study. Another explanation is linked to the worsening of the economic situation: the progressive drying-up of financial resources may account, at least to some extent, for the lethargy of sociological research in subsequent years. In addition, with the deteriorating economic situation, social security problems were becoming politically highly sensitive and governments were reluctant to finance academic research the results of which they could not control.

## The revival in the 1980s: the quest for rationalisation

The next noticeable revival of the interest in the sociology of social security on the academic ground may be witnessed in the early 1980s. Organised by RC19 in collaboration with ISSA, a meeting on the 'Sociology of Social Security: Innovation and Change' was held, in June 1984, at the University of Bergen (Norway). Close to 50 participants from 15 countries took part in the discussions.[5] Convened in a period when social security systems were under pressure in most countries, the central question asked was how to change the system in order to make it perform better and with the greatest economy of resources. But, as most people agreed, without a precise knowledge of the functioning of the system and of the impact it had on society, there was no way of saying which changes were preferable. Accordingly, several papers focused on subjects such as distributional effects of different kinds of social security benefits, while others dealt with decision making within the social security system and with the political forces influencing the future of social security. In addition, the earlier-quoted important paper by Sigg (1986) reviewed the past and present efforts in this field and set up some pointers for the future.

We have already drawn attention to the difficulties involved in the sociological research of social security. These have been pointed out much more forcefully by the organiser of the Bergen meeting, Else Oyen, in her editorial introduction to the meeting papers, which were published in *International Sociology*:

> The system of social security is difficult to penetrate for outsiders in any country. Due to the complexity of the rules of allocation, expert language, use of discretion and principles of confidentiality, the system is inaccessible for researchers and clients alike. It takes years to understand the system well enough to make it an object of research. The complexity of the system and the diversity of its relationships with other parts of society make it difficult to establish theories of a more general nature. Politicians and administrators of the system have not been eager to ask for research, which might raise questions about the value of social security as an adequate instrument of social policy. It was not until the so-called 'crisis' of the welfare state came into focus that the social security system became an interesting object of research. Social security being the back-bone of the welfare state, there is no understanding of the welfare state without some understanding of the functions of the social security system. (Oyen, 1986, p 219)

The conclusion is at hand: technical difficulties apart, sociology discovered social security as an object of research during a period of plenty that witnessed its greatest institutional expansion, with a view to contributing to the orientation of its future development. It has rediscovered it some 20 years later, during a period of decline caused by the adverse economic situation of society, with a view either to defend it or to help with the retrenchment of the institution. Manifestly, both technical and material conditions of societal environment play an important role in this change of focus.

Another sign of the reviving interest in the subject was the 1984 Symposium of the European Institute for Social Security, which adopted as its main theme 'Sociological Research and Social Security' (EISS, 1986). The meeting, convened in Luxembourg, was meant to bring together researchers and practitioners to discuss the results of sociological research in different fields of direct interest to social security. The meaning of 'sociological research' was taken in a very broad sense and a wide range of specialists, including lawyers and actuaries, presented contributions in the form of specific sectoral studies or national monographs.

The second international seminar on the sociology of social security was held in June 1989 at the University of Edinburgh. Convened again under the joint auspices of ISSA and RC19, it was attended by some 70 participants from 15 countries, presenting 28 papers. These were discussed under five headings:

- the objectives of social security;
- social security and the labour market;
- social security and gender;
- the administration of social security;
- the state of social security research.

In the words of the organisers, the quality of the papers reflected the growing emergence of a distinctive sociology of social security in the intervening five years since the Bergen seminar. To the extent that a number of contributions presented to the seminar were destined for publication elsewhere, only 15 papers were included in the volume published under the title *The Sociology of Social Security*, which appeared two years later, accompanied by a very extensive bibliography (Adler et al, 1991). This book contains only a few general conceptual papers – most of the contributions are sectoral papers dealing with specific branches or aspects of social security or with particular countries.

The introductory chapter, written by four members of the University of Edinburgh (Michael Adler, Colin Bell, Jochen Clasen and Adrian Sinfield) examines at some length what the authors call the 'non-emergence of the sociology of social security' and throws some interesting light on the subject observed from the academic platform. Thus, for instance, with regard to the UK, this may be partly attributed to the impact of:

> an early bifurcation between the concerns of sociological theory and those of empirical social investigation which eventually led to the establishment of separate Departments of Sociology and Departments of Social Administration (later called Departments of Social Policy) in certain Universities. (Adler et al, 1991, p 3)

Another important element in this analysis is the role of research funding, which depends largely on government policy in this field. Due to these priorities, the 'focus has been on contemporary, problem-related research rather than on historical or comparative research, and on multi-disciplinary research rather than research from the perspective of a single discipline' (Adler et al, 1991, p 5). This last observation only confirms the research orientation noted in the early 1970s in the international activities of ISSA.

The authors ascribe the increased interest in sociological research on social security in the late 1980s to economic and social developments, which affected the income security of a large part of the population. A growing number of one-parent families, the impact of demographic changes, especially with regard to the increasing number of retired people, and high levels and long spells of unemployment were among these factors. In discussing the contributions that contemporary sociology could make to the understanding of social security, the authors suggested grouping them under six headings:

- *A sociological definition of social security* should help to overcome substantial national variations in the ways in which social security is defined in social legislation and constitute a basis for a functional comparison of social security provisions.
- *A sociological characterisation of social security systems* should enable an adequate understanding of social security by an appropriate analysis of their salient features, be it in terms of classical administrative categories or in terms of relationships used for the classification of welfare states.
- *Comparative studies of the origins and development of social security systems* contribute by an identification and examination of different social factors behind such developments.
- *Macro-sociological studies of the impact of social security on social stratification* reveal more complex repercussions of certain social provisions on the population and on various forms of socially reproduced inequalities in society.
- *Micro-sociological studies of the experience of social security* provide a necessary complement to macro-sociological assessments of the impact of social security by showing how receiving benefits affects people's attitudes and behaviour.
- *Sociological studies of the administration of social security* should fill an important gap in sociological research regarding the routine forms of administrative decision making and the relationships between the administration and social security beneficiaries.

Notwithstanding the rather optimistic outlook adopted by the organisers of the Edinburgh conference with regard to future studies in the field of the sociology of social security, their optimism was not borne out by facts and there was no follow-up on that meeting. It seems significant and characteristic of the situation in these years, that when a highly important event took place at the University of York in 1992, that is, an international conference entitled 'Social Security 50 Years after Beveridge', one of the sessions was devoted to 'The economics of social security', another to 'Comparative studies of social security', but the sociology of social security as a subject was missing from the agenda.

## The final pattern: sociological studies of social policy and welfare

A number of reasons may explain why no other international seminar on the subject was organised after Edinburgh. Some of them have already been mentioned previously in relation to the initial decline in the 1970s, and among these, the political sensitivity and the lack of research funds would no doubt continue to hold true. Furthermore, the already-noted preference in government-financed projects for problem-oriented and multidisciplinary research still applies. This alone may account to a large extent for the absence of any new initiative on the part of large international organisations with competence in the field of social security.

Among the professional sociologists the change noted earlier by Sigg (1986), which consisted in replacing initial macro-sociological studies of social security with studies of global or sectoral social policies, or of the welfare state, was later fully reflected in the activities of the main professional body, the RC19 of the ISA. It was this committee that broadly covered and no doubt continues to cover the need for exchanges such as those at Bergen or Edinburgh. Hence, a follow-up on what has been described in these pages would amount to writing a history of trends in RC19's scientific interests and activities. This is not the ambition of this book and we shall limit ourselves to only a few remarks regarding more recent developments.

It seems appropriate to highlight in this context the growing importance of comparative studies of social security. The search for rationalisation of social protection policies and procedures points directly to the need for comparing different national experiences in this field. It is worth noting that, particularly within the EU and as a result of its enlargement process, what used to be a simple exchange of experience offered to all interested parties, has now become a search for 'good practices', or at least what may appear as such to the expert. Similarly, the highly fashionable subject of 'convergence' of social policy developments at the European level was examined in recent years from many different angles but without any conclusive findings.

With regard to ISSA, which has always considered exchange of experience as its veritable raison d'être, a major effort went into the preparation of a research symposium on international comparisons of social security policies and systems, organised by the 'Mission Interministérielle Recherche Expérimentation (MIRE)' of the French Government in June 1990 in Paris (MIRE-ISSA, 1992). The intention of the organisers was to make a global survey of the comparative art and to discuss characteristics and issues of comparative research as well as methodological problems at the worldwide level. In subsequent years, MIRE pursued its ambitious research programme in a series entitled 'Comparing social welfare systems in Europe' while ISSA continued its tradition of periodic research conferences, the most recent of which were devoted to 'Social Security in a Long Life Society' (Antwerp 2003) and 'Labour Market and Social Security' (Warsaw 2007).

In the following chapter we propose to examine in more detail the preoccupations of the early period of ISSA activities in the field of the sociology of social security, as described in these pages. Before doing so, a brief assessment of the importance of this work in a historical perspective may be of interest. As indicated earlier (p 69), among the areas of contemporary research singled out by the authors of the Edinburgh volume on the sociology of social security (Adler et al, 1991, p 9), one deals with 'comparative studies of the origins and development of social security systems'. My own sociological factor analysis (Rys, 1964), described as 'pioneering work', is mentioned there together with the well-known study by Esping-Andersen (1990) on the three worlds of welfare capitalism. Comparing the approaches used in these two studies, it would appear that during the 25 years that separate them, the stones, bricks and other building materials were put together to construct model houses. The fact that Esping-Andersen's typology has met with such a resounding echo seems to indicate that at the time of its publication there was a badly felt need for some sensible classification of the existing welfare systems, providing a framework for a better understanding of their functions in the light of their historical development. In a more recent study, Peter Taylor-Gooby (2002, p 602) suggests that Esping-Andersen's work attracted widespread attention because it 'integrated economic, social and political accounts of the development of welfare systems'. In his view 'recent approaches to state welfare have in common that they are sensitive to the interaction of economic, social and political factors in welfare state stability and change, and are aware that all these dimensions must be taken into account'. This was precisely the message

# FIVE

# A macro-sociological approach to the study of social security

The historical survey of the sociology of social security outlined in the previous chapter has underlined the growing importance of comparative studies of social policy. This seems natural because the tools of a sociological analysis can only be developed and tested when applied to several societies. My own factor analysis presented in this chapter and developed as part of the research programme of ISSA in Geneva was directly conceived as a methodological tool for a comparative study.

## Presentation of an early forerunner of macro-sociological factor analysis

This reference goes back to my unpublished doctoral thesis, written in the middle of 1950s. The title was 'Sécurité sociale en France et en Grande-Bretagne – etude sociologique' and the viva voce was held at the Sorbonne in February 1958. Its purpose was to study, at the international level and on a comparative basis, the interrelations between the institution of social security and its societal environment. This implied examining, first, how the institution was conceived and implemented in each country and, second, what were the main factors shaping its subsequent development. The underlying philosophical approach was holistic, assuming a full interconnection of social phenomena.

The sociological analysis included demographic, economic, political and psychological factors, studied within the context of each country. The psychological factor was included in the analysis more as a reminder of what was missing to complete the exercise, rather than as an account of some already available evidence. The argument in favour of including it was based on the observation that in current political life, assumptions are often made about what people wish for in social security without providing the necessary proof. Another point of interest concerned the difference in attitudes depending on personal experience with the working of the institution; a person who had actually received some social security benefits would not feel the same way as a passive participant in the scheme. At the time of writing, no serious sociological study was available on the subject on either side of the Channel, and an overview was presented of several projects under way approaching, at least marginally, user surveys and public opinion enquiries.

The notion of path dependency was touched on in this thesis by the concept of the 'typical reaction of society to the problem of indigence of its members', considered as part of the national character. It was observed that in Great Britain it was the duty of the state to provide for indigent members of society, and this principle ran throughout the history of social protection from the Poor Law to the Beveridge Report. In contrast with this, the situation in France revealed a quasi-permanent discrepancy between theory and practice; while the legal theory aimed at transferring the overall responsibility to the state, in practice, due to the individualistic approach prevailing in public life, this led to decentralised provisions and self-administered social insurance schemes.

The overall conclusion of the study was that the development of social security was dependent essentially on the distribution of political power in society, on the strength of different pressure groups and on the relations between the state and different components of civil society.

## The stages of maturation

The first opportunity to present the sociological factor analysis on an international platform was offered by the Fourteenth National Congress of Sociology, organised by the Mexican Sociological Association and the Mexican Social Insurance Institute (MSII) in November 1963 in Culiacan (Mexico). The geographical location of this event may be surprising, but it is easily understandable in the context of that time. Mexico, which had launched its social security programme in 1943 (with the help of the ILO located during wartime in Montreal) developed in the post-war years an extremely dynamic concept of social security, providing not only cash benefits for specific contingencies but also social services of all kinds representing a real social development programme. The political power of the MSII was such that for a politician occupying the post of the Director General, the next higher step could only be the office of the President of the country. It was hence logical for such an institution to appear as spearhead of the innovative social research. Inevitably, given the particular scope of the institution, the papers presented to the congress covered a vast range of subjects, from demographic aspects of social security,[1] to relations between social security and architecture, to the importance of pre-marriage savings.

The timing of this congress undoubtedly speeded up the finalisation of my own study on sociology of social security, published a few months later in the *Bulletin of the ISSA* (Rys, 1964). The fact that the study was available in the four working languages of ISSA (English, French, Spanish and German) contributed considerably to its wide diffusion and, within two years, specialised social security journals in different countries completed the worldwide distribution in a dozen other languages. Manifestly, the professional circles were in need of some coherent conceptual presentation of social security in order to interpret its recent developments. It is this particular reception received by the study that may make it worth attention.

The purpose of the paper was 'to give a broad outline of one of the ways in which social security can be studied by sociologists as a social institution playing an important role in modern society' (Rys, 1964, p 3). It was hence an invitation to join active research rather than a blueprint to follow. From the very beginning, the object of the exercise was narrowed down in line with the observation that 'the same set of conditions which permits the establishment of a social insurance scheme in a country generally also determines the shape of the scheme adopted and its evolution over a period of time' (p 3). This pointed clearly to the need for analysing what we now call path dependence in terms of sociological factors, which can explain it.

A particular conceptual difficulty of sociological factor analysis lies in the fact that it deals at any given time with the same societal environment, with each factor representing only a different aspect of the same reality. But these aspects are interrelated and, in a constantly changing societal environment, their relationships change. Consequently, the impact of each aspect of the total environment on a social institution, considered as a sociological factor, can only be studied in its manifestations over a period of time.

The most important advancement in sociological factor analysis presented in the 1964 paper concerned the division into *endogenous* and *exogenous* factors. The holistic concept of the study recognising the permanent interpenetration of various factors commanded a more careful terminology – hence the suggestion to think in terms of 'predominantly internal' and 'predominantly external' factors. It is clear that to the extent that no modern society can live in isolation from its neighbours, most internal factors will be subject to some influence coming from outside, and, inversely, most external factors will start their existence within one particular society, before they acquire an international influence.

Another conceptual advance concerns the introduction of *the institutional evolution factor.* This refers to the effects of practical experience, gained in the course of the administration of a social security scheme, on further evolution of the institution. In this concept, the institution becomes, in the long run, one of the determining factors of its own further development. The emphasis in the paper was on the importance of national experience for the performance of a scheme. This was in line with the results of some contemporary studies, indicating that the length of national experience with the running of a social security scheme was an important variable in studies on welfare expenditure (Aaron, 1963). This was also as far as we could get towards the notion of 'path dependency', a much broader concept developed in more recent years.

Last but not least, considerable attention was paid to the *reciprocal impact* of social security on society. It is only natural that a study dealing with the working of a social institution in its societal environment will take into account not only how the institution is conditioned by the existing societal forces and their interrelations, but also how this institution, once under way, influences in turn the different aspects of its original environment. This concept is of considerable importance, since it represents one of the ways to measure the attainment of its objectives.

The text that follows contains a number of further amendments resulting from the use of this material in lectures delivered to an undergraduate course, organised by the Social Policy Institute of the Charles' University in Prague, during the period from 1991 to 1996. These lectures were subsequently published under the title 'Theory and practice of comparative studies in the field of social security' in a special volume devoted to this course (Munkova, 2004, pp 11-46). I have also used the macro-sociological factor analysis for explaining social security reforms in the post-communist Czech Republic, which took place during the years 1993 to 1995 (Rys, 1999). The transition countries of Central Europe offered a particularly propitious ground for this exercise following the fall of their totalitarian regimes in the late 1980s. Of particular interest was the opportunity to study the differential speed of transformation of political institutions as compared with social protection systems within one country and between the countries concerned. Finally, in a concise way, I have applied this analytical approach to social security developments in the Czech Republic, Hungary and Poland in a short study, which is briefly summarised in the next chapter (Rys, 2002).

# The macro-sociological factor analysis of social security and its use

The main purpose of this method of study is to go beyond the descriptive account of the institution as contained in legislative texts and to explain why it is organised the way it is and why it functions the way it does. This knowledge is essential for the politician, legislator and decision maker in guiding the development of the institution – it is important to know whether a proposed reform follows the established path and stands a better chance of being accepted, or whether and to what degree it departs from the existing concepts and requires a more important effort in explaining it to the public. But it is equally useful to all actors involved in the implementation of the legislation, including the agents of the institution whose task it is to interpret the legislative rules for all the beneficiaries. If the knowledge of the historical evolution of the institution in a country and of the concepts used helps to improve correct interpretation of texts, the knowledge of the forces that are at work in shaping social security legislation helps to understand the function of the institution in society.

The reason for seeking information beyond the purely descriptive level is best demonstrated by many comparative tables and classifications. A general survey may indicate to a reader interested in family allowances that both France and Great Britain have established a nationwide system of family allowances. But only a deeper analysis will explain to them that while in France this was traditionally one of the pillars of social policy, in Great Britain it was more of a residual measure, originally opposed by trades unions on account of dividing the wage-earners. Similarly, descriptive materials will show that both Denmark and Switzerland have national systems of health insurance; but only a more thorough study will reveal that while in Denmark this is a universal state-financed system administered at the local government level, in Switzerland it is basically a cantonal legislative arrangement relying on privately operated health funds. It is hence clear that any superficial handling of this type of data is counterproductive and that a correct understanding of the functions of social security measures is indispensable for any meaningful comparative study.

Lastly, the factor analysis is also of importance for an assessment of the institution's performance and of its capacity to reach its objectives. In concrete terms, this will concern its capacity to redress a declining birth rate through a significant grant of family allowances, to reduce poverty in old age through a well-functioning general pension scheme or to improve the health of the population through an efficient health insurance. And this will also include its potential for improving economic conditions of society, a truth that was well known in previous decades, and which has only recently been rediscovered following a number of mistakes made in the overall governance of society.

## Internal factors of macro-sociological analysis

As mentioned earlier, these factors belong to the internal environment of any particular society, and are identified as such, although they are inevitably exposed to external influences. This interdependence justifies the precaution of always thinking in terms of *predominantly* internal or external factors. At the internal factors level, the macro–sociological analysis is using the specific approach of several social sciences, including its own, to bring to light a number of basic components of a given societal environment and their influence on the institution. Thus, we come to distinguish the impact of demographic, economic, sociological and political factors with varying levels or degrees of influence.

It is also possible to recognise certain hierarchical relationships between individual factors. This follows from the very nature of the institution and its genesis as an end product of a legislative process. To the extent that laws are prepared by ministerial authorities, organs of political power, and discussed and voted upon by deputies representing political parties, it is obvious that the principal role belongs to the political factor. Even the influence of what we may call 'hard factors', relating to demographic and economic conditions of society, has to pass through the screen of the political evaluation undertaken by legislators to become effective. The same is true about the sociological factor, dealing with pressures developed by various interest groups, and about all external factors. This inevitably leads to the conclusion that in a democratic society, institutional structures of social security and their development depend, in the last analysis, on the global perception and evaluation by the policy maker of all factors involved.

### The demographic factor

Every social institution is directly influenced by the composition and characteristics of the population groups it is expected to serve. This is particularly true about social security, which considers the demographic structure of the population as one of its basic parameters. Consequently, we have to turn to demography or some of its branches for the necessary data.

Following the usual scientific division, *quantitative demography* will provide information on the physiological basis of the institution. Since one of the functional consequences of social security is the redistribution of income between certain categories of the population, the relation between the young and the old, the healthy and the sick, or between the number of families and that of single people, will play a significant role in the development of the institution.

In a social insurance scheme, these data will be of fundamental importance for actuarial calculations destined to ensure financial equilibrium of the scheme by a correct assessment of contributions and benefits. During a period when population ageing is one of the most important challenges of all pension funds, the knowledge of demographic projections regarding this question will be a key to understanding the pension policy adopted in a country. On the other side of the life cycle, the birth rate figures may help to explain the policy of a country in the field of family allowances.

Two subdivisions of *qualitative demography* will be of direct interest for a macro-sociological factor analysis of social security. *Economic demography*, which explores the relationship between population and economy, will thus provide information on the evolution of unemployment, a problem of fundamental interest for the financial equilibrium of the institution. Studies on the family and labour market will throw important light on the family policy in a country and all connecting welfare services, while studies on the economic impact of the long-term decline in mortality will help to understand the evolution of pension schemes. The information provided by *social demography* on specific population aspects of society will explain the presence of strong unified schemes in countries with a large industrial population, while the political and social importance of certain occupational groups (for example in agriculture and mining) will be reflected in the existence of a number of occupational schemes. Investigations of special arrangements for the benefit of students, artists or clergy will also use data provided by this branch of science.

Regarding the reciprocal impact of the institution on demography, we shall examine the possible influence on the birth rate of family allowances paid at a high rate and for a prolonged period of time. A well-functioning pension scheme should positively influence the longevity of the population and universal health insurance coverage should help to maintain a productive workforce. Appropriate employment promotion measures will contribute to keeping unemployment figures within acceptable limits. All these effects have been well known in the past but the tendency to use them in public debates has naturally varied according to the political colour of the government. The new element intervening in recent years has been the improvement of methods measuring this impact in economic terms.

## The economic factor

The principal technique of social security – social insurance – operates not only a certain degree of redistribution of income among specific population groups, but also a spread of income over an individual's lifetime. Since income is the key word, it follows that the economic situation of society – the generator of income – will be of primary importance. Financial resources needed to maintain a minimum income for people who have fallen victim to various social risks can only be provided from the product of work of the economically active population. It is on their productivity that the level of all social security benefits will depend in the long run.

The importance of economic prosperity for the advancement of social security has been confirmed in recent decades when a significant slowdown in the growth of national income combined with a rapid extension of mass unemployment marked a turning point in the expansion of the European welfare state. But this does not permit us to formulate a general rule that it is in time of plenty that social insurance will make most advances, while a period of economic recession is likely to be synonymous with stagnation. All throughout human history we have seen social security get its impetus in periods of most adverse economic circumstances caused by wars and other types of social crises. Typically, it was the period after the First World War that saw a considerable expansion of social insurance, and it was during the Second World War that the concept of social security was born. This seems to indicate that it is the political motivation arising out of an adverse economic situation that is the determining element, not the economic situation itself.

Similarly, the level of economic development in a country is not necessarily indicative of the degree of development of a social security scheme. Indeed, some of the most industrialised and prosperous countries such as the US or Japan will not be found among the leading promoters of the welfare state. Again, other factors must be at work to obtain the optimum situation for the growth of the institution. And when we turn our attention to low-income countries, the same picture will emerge. We only have to quote the already-mentioned shining example of Mexico in the 1960s to realise that even low- or medium-income countries can make extraordinary achievements. We must hence conclude that there is no uniform relationship between the state of the national economy and the degree of social insurance provisions. Manifestly, the political ideology or the government's will to act seems to be the overriding element.

Although the economic factor may not be the main force in the development process of social security, it is, nevertheless, the most significant element of societal environment to determine the limits of its development at any given time. In this respect, the main question is, what constitutes the limits of national economic outlay on social security? Many people will argue that in our present consumer society where a great number of individuals are prepared to spend a considerable part of their revenue on cars or home electronics, the limits of social security contributions are not yet in sight. On the other hand, the supporters of neoliberal economic theory will maintain that these limits were reached a long time ago and that this is precisely the reason for the present economic slowdown. But these are probably extreme views, which point to the need for searching for a new consensus somewhere in between. Whatever side we may take, the reply to the question on acceptable limits of social security expenditure can only be given by a democratic discussion on societal choices.

The impact of the national economy on social security is not uniform, nor is the influence of social security on the economy. If, on the one hand, it may increase production costs of enterprises that have to compete in global markets with low-labour-cost countries, it does, on the other hand, augment consumption, since social security benefits do not increase savings. As in the above case, the evaluation of the reciprocal impact of social security on the economy is unlikely to meet with unanimity, since it is the ideological and political view of the situation that determines the attitude. Nevertheless, it may be considered as a sign of the times that lessons have been learned in recent history and many circles, which until now considered the institution as an economic evil, may now admit its positive sides. Once again, progress in this direction will depend to a large extent on the capacity to prove this positive effect by an appropriate cost-benefit analysis. Contrary to the situation in the 1960s, courses on the 'economics of social security' are regularly proposed in many universities and the impact of social security on savings or on labour supply is one of their permanent features.

### *The sociological factor*

The study of this factor concerns primarily social actors involved in policy formulation and operations of social security. It will be of particular importance for the understanding of the institutional development in countries having adopted the so-called corporatist model such as Austria, France or Germany where *social partners*, that is, trades unions and employers' federations, collaborate in the management of the institution.

Another focus of attention will be on *interest* or *pressure groups*, which play a role in the implementation of social security provisions or represent the beneficiaries. Among the former, the most active are the professional organisations of doctors who provide medical care within the framework of health insurance. The influence of the medical profession is particularly strong in view of its importance in the everyday life of individuals and also of its representation in competent legislative bodies. The most important pressure groups on the user side of the institution are associations of old-age pensioners who may in some countries adopt and even formally assume the function of a political party. Other groups worthy of attention may be found among the organisations representing disabled people, war veterans, associations working for the promotion of family and so on. It is clear that most pressure groups exercise their influence through actions aimed at political parties.

Another influential group of actors with direct interest in social security is at work in what is known as the *social economy sector*. This concept was originally developed in France, where it represents essentially cooperative societies of social character, mutual benefit societies working mainly in the field of health, charities and other public utility organisations. Included are also voluntary pension funds established at the occupational or enterprise level. The common denominator of all these organisations is economic activity on a non-profit-making basis, aimed at improving the social conditions of life. They hence complement the functions of the statutory social security arrangements and as such have a long-term impact on the development of the institution. This sector is the object of particular attention within the EU, on account of its potential role in alleviating the financial burden of state social welfare measures.

Needless to say, the existing *private insurance sector* will be of interest in studying social insurance developments in many countries. Apart from sharing a common basic technique of the trade, this sector is expected to take over part of the social insurance functions at times when the amount of obligatory contributions for state provisions is considered excessive. The last decades of the 20th century produced an enormous amount of literature on the relationship between public and private arrangements and this interest has weakened only in more recent years, following the demonstration of the precarious nature of private investments in financial markets. But it would be a mistake to believe that the delimitation of frontiers between the public and private sector only leads to the definition of respective shares of a given volume of expenditure. Instances may be quoted from the history of pension provisions, when the introduction of a new social security measure led in a short time to the expansion of private insurance, simply due to the increase in the level of public awareness of the problem of providing for old age.

### *The political factor*

From its very origins, the history of social security shows that it is not enough to have an adequate technique to implement a plan; the most important thing is to have the political will and means to introduce it. The social insurance technique was known from the end of the 17th century, but only the chancellor Bismarck succeeded in having a scheme adopted nearly 200 years later. The presence of the political will to act is hence the decisive element for the introduction of any social institution and the analysis of the whole process leading to its enactment is necessary for a full understanding of the institution's organisation, structure and functions. It is obvious that this process takes place against the background of the basic reaction of society to the problem of the destitution of its members and that this reaction is related to world trends in the field of social policy, often under the influence of certain political ideologies.

Another historical lesson concerns the fact that many social security schemes are launched at times of an intensive feeling of national solidarity, resulting from the experience of a serious menace to individual existence such as a war or a deep economic or political crisis. Subsequent development is influenced by specific interests of different population groups expressed through the intermediary of existing political parties. When the institution reaches a certain degree of development, the classical cliché assuming that left-wing parties vote in support and right-wing parties oppose it, ceases to hold true. Moreover, as has been shown in the course of comparative studies, every country has in this field its own dynamics; as a result, it is possible to find cases where a right-wing party in one country is in a position to propose measures that a left-wing party in another country has not yet dared to include in its programme.

Political parties formulate their social policy programme in line with their ideological concepts regarding the governance of society; as far as the social security programme is concerned, this will be basically determined by their judgement as to what extent the cover against social risks should be a matter for collective provisions, or for private arrangements left to the individual. In practical political life they have to pay attention to the preferences expressed by their electors as well as to the positions adopted by other actors involved in the decision-making process. The institutional development of social security in a democratic society is the result of successive and often contradictory political decisions by governments coming to power at different times and favouring different aspects of social protection policy.

Political parties implement their policies within the framework provided by the political system of the country, which exercises considerable influence on the institutional structure and content of social protection. The history of social security shows that political democracy as such does not lead automatically to the adoption of social protection laws. On the contrary, the developments that took place in the course of recent decades indicate that totalitarian regimes, right wing or left wing, may be capable of introducing social security measures and using or abusing them with greater ease than democracy. This is a logical consequence of the fact that in a totalitarian system there is no need for playing an arbiter between conflicting interests of different population groups. However, as demonstrated earlier, the quality of a social security scheme does not depend only on the degree of the material existence guaranteed to the individual; it depends above all on the human quality of the individual's existence in a society.

Knowledge of the structure of political institutions and the way they function in different countries is important for an understanding of their respective social protection systems. A recent comparative study has shown very clearly the influence of institutional structures in Canada, France and Switzerland on their respective social security systems (Berra, 2000). It seems obvious that a centrally administered country such as France will not adopt the same approach to the organisation of social security as a country with provincial administration such as Canada, or a confederation of the Swiss type.

Even the way in which a country prepares and reforms its social legislation plays an important role. Most Western democracies proceed with great care in view of the high degree of political sensibility to any intervention in the operations of social security. In the case of a major reform the Anglo-Saxon tradition would require the establishment of a special committee and the publication of its report. This may also be the case in a country with a corporative model of the French type, but in this case, every reform needs a preliminary negotiation with social partners. The situation is even more complicated in a country practising direct democracy, such as Switzerland, where nearly every proposal of social legislation, after adoption by the government and the parliament, becomes the object of a national referendum requested by its opponents. In this way, direct democracy becomes a factor, which may slow down the development of social security in a country.

A special phenomenon regarding the relationship between the system of government and social security could be observed in the closing years of the 20th century in most post-communist countries in Central Europe. Although technically the political system represented a fully functioning democracy, social security reforms of fundamental importance were being passed practically without any major public discussion. This was due mainly to the fact that neither the politicians nor the expert circles in the country had sufficient knowledge of the working of the schemes that were being introduced to replace the communist state social security system. Under these circumstances, the hardly existing civil society, still in the process of formation, and the general public, accustomed to receiving laws from above without much questioning, played a very passive role. The result was a reform process by trial and error that only much later came to reach the democratic consensus-seeking level, in line with the advancing knowledge acquired by all actors involved.

## External factors of macro-sociological analysis

It may be appropriate to stress once again that this type of sociological factor analysis can be meaningful only to the extent that we admit from the outset that, most of the time, there is no clear-cut division between internal and external factors and that these categories interpenetrate each other in the societal environment of the institution. But there is what may objectively be recognised as a predominantly internal or external basis of factors under study, and this in itself is helpful for a better understanding of social security developments in a country.

With this qualification in mind, in this section it is proposed to study under the above heading international cultural transfers relating to social security. Taking into account the specific knowledge basis of the institution, it may be useful to treat the diffusion of ideas and techniques of social protection separately from the media and the means used for this purpose. The knowledge transfer will be dealt with here irrespective of whether it takes place occasionally or permanently, spontaneously or in an organised manner, although this could possibly give rise to another sub-classification of external influences. Should these criteria be retained, the activities of specialised international organisations discussed under this heading would represent the most effective external factor, the knowledge being diffused both permanently and in an organised way.

## *Ideas, ideologies, laws and techniques of social protection*

Certain countries developed at specific times in their history a special effort in this field, serving later to guide many others. Thus, it is possible to point in this context to medieval Spain laying foundations for a social doctrine, which influenced even centuries later the whole continent of Latin America. The French Revolution was another powerful source of inspiration for social thinking, leading from the notion of equality of citizens to that of social justice. And it would be superfluous to deal at length with the influence of the Beveridge Report. These ideas produced by important national thinkers or generated by social movements of their time were spreading through normal channels of cultural transfers as much as ideas pertaining to other spheres of human activity. At other times, for instance with regard to spreading the state social security concept adopted in the Soviet Union, the means of diffusion may have been more coercive. In both cases, it is important for the student of the history of social security in a country to locate the influence that may have been exercised by these models.

The historical development of social security law will take us from the formulation of the right of the poor to social assistance in the 18th century, to the right of the workers to social insurance recognised in the second half of the 19th century, and to end up with the declaration of social security being an indivisible part of human rights at the end of the Second World War. From then onwards, the development of international social security law at the worldwide level has been one of the chief tasks of the ILO in Geneva. Among the main instruments of this endeavour is the standard-setting activity of the ILO, seeking to raise the level of protection by means of ratification of international conventions. Among the regional supranational organisations, the EU plays an important role; although it abandons to its member states the responsibility for determining their own social protection policy, certain aspects of it, for example with regard to the social rights of migrant workers or the equality of men and women, will be subject to common rules. The governmental international organisations will not be the only actors in this field. The legal profession will contribute to the scientific progress, for instance, through the activities of the International Society for Labour and Social Security Law. In analysing the social security scheme in a country it will be important to know what measures are imposed by membership of a supranational entity, or, in the case of a developing country, which international organisation provided the technical assistance to help with the introduction of a scheme or with some major reform.

With regard to the development of social protection techniques, as has been pointed out earlier in this book, a permanent stumbling block of the early period was the technical incapacity to finance and administer a scheme on a nationwide basis. It is only with the advent of social insurance that governments obtained an instrument for securing the material existence of their citizens by means of the redistribution of income over an individual's lifetime as well as between different income groups and generations. During the first half of the 20th century the technicians of social insurance were essentially lawyers and actuaries – the former to give the institution a legal structure and the latter to organise sustainable financial flows so as to make it work. With the expansion of social security after the Second World War, other professionals, mainly economists and sociologists, joined in to collaborate on the development of the concepts necessary for further advancement of the institution.

It should be borne in mind that the notion of progress in social protection techniques covers not only the general management of nationwide systems but also specific measures within individual branches of social security. Thus, for instance, the capitation fee in medical care, the so-called splitting of state pensions for married couples, or transferability of occupational pension rights – all these are examples of the advancement of techniques put at the disposal of the insured population and spreading from one country to another. In more recent years, the introduction of the 'notional individual account' in the Swedish pension system so as to integrate into the pension formula elements reflecting the evolution of the economic situation has attracted wide attention and has been copied by other countries. On the other hand, the general development, still under way, that consists of replacing defined benefit pension schemes with defined contribution arrangements, while certainly representing a technical innovation, can hardly be viewed as advancement.

### *Media and means of knowledge transfers in social security*

If we start with spontaneous cultural transfers, the first media to be mentioned will be *university teaching and academic exchanges.* Although it is difficult to trace from one case to another, or to provide some quantitative assessment of their influence, the long-term impact on the 'social security doctrine' of personalities such as T. H. Marshall or Richard Titmuss can hardly be questioned. It is only exceptionally that the lesson may be brought home with a concrete example. Thus, for instance, a student of the history of social insurance in Costa Rica, struck by a relatively advanced model used in its launching stage, will understand the situation better when they learn that one of its founders studied in the Belgian University of Louvain. And in the long term, if we observe the extraordinary development of comparative studies, can anybody reasonably doubt that the exercise of this discipline does not contribute to the cross-fertilisation of knowledge about social security?

Another perhaps less important but equally significant means of diffusing knowledge is the *migration of experts.* This was quite common in the Middle Ages and after with respect to university teachers and we are hence not surprised to learn from history books that the first manual of public assistance to the poor, destined for the Belgian town of Bruges, was written in 1526 by a Spanish humanist and professor at Louvain University, Jean Louis Vives, driven out of his country by the inquisition. Closer to our time, we can refer to the case of Jewish scientists fleeing in the late 1930s Central Europe and Nazi Germany. The public is well aware of the contribution made to the development of Western sciences by personalities such as Freud and Einstein, but hardly anyone would be able to point to the work of outstanding actuaries, such as professors Schönbaum of Czechoslovakia and Thullen of Germany who have great merits for the development of social insurance schemes in Latin America. In fact this latter migration case could be extended to cover the wartime transfer of the International Labour Office from Geneva to Montreal; since Latin America remained freely accessible to ILO experts, many countries in the region could benefit from their presence to launch their social insurance schemes.

An extremely influential vehicle for the diffusion of knowledge of social security is *political ideology.* It is common knowledge that during the period between the First and Second World Wars in Europe, it was essentially the social democratic parties that were promoting social insurance as a means of improving the situation of workers. In Part One of this book the influence of the communist and neoliberal ideologies on social security were discussed at some length. The obvious difficulty lies in identifying what part of the social protection doctrine defended by a national party comes from outside and what part is of local origin, possibly due to some path dependency. In most cases, due to the complexity of national legislations and the need for an adaptation to the local situation, the external influence provides an inspiration but not a blueprint for a social security scheme.

History has often highlighted another powerful external factor, resulting from *colonisation or territorial occupation* after a war. Whoever had to deal with social security schemes in developing countries will recognise the extraordinary impact of colonisation on the system adopted in a newly independent country. A typical example is provided by French-speaking African countries, which, shortly after independence in the 1960s, started creating the least suitable branch of social security from the point of view of their needs and priorities, that is, family allowances. The reason for this was the existence in their territories of family allowance funds paying benefits to members of the French colonial administration. The governments of these new countries rightly considered that it was in their interest to make use of the administrative skills of these funds first to extend the benefits to their own citizens and later to entrust them with the administration of other branches of social insurance. It is interesting to note that this transformation process was smoother and speedier than in the English-speaking countries in Africa and Asia, formerly under the British administration. The latter had introduced in their territories the system of Provident funds based not on the principle of insurance but on that of obligatory savings. When the time came to start thinking about transformation and the introduction of social insurance, the task proved to be much more difficult than in the case of their French-speaking neighbours.

Regarding the impact of territorial occupation on social security schemes, the case of Soviet Union has already been mentioned, which exported its model after the Second World War to countries in Central and Eastern Europe, temporarily occupied by the Red Army. The transmission was made effective through the imposition of a political ideology and enacted in each country by the ruling Communist Party. But the classical historical example is that of the French territory of Alsace-Lorraine that had been attached to the German Empire from 1871 to 1918. This meant that Bismarck's social insurance laws introduced between 1883 and 1889 fully applied in this region, which thus gained a considerable advance over France. So much so that when the territory returned to France after the First World War, the French government did not consider it politically feasible to abolish the

German system and maintained its functions with some modifications, allowing Alsace-Lorraine to enjoy a special status within the French national scheme. Needless to say, the experience of this regional scheme served as an inspiration to the French legislator when the country decided to launch its new social security system in 1945.

## *The impact of international organisations*

Since the Second World War, the diffusion and improvement of knowledge regarding the organisation and functions of social security and its institutional promotion has become the object of systematic and organised efforts on the part of several international organisations. The impact of their work naturally differs according to the status of the organisation and the importance given to social security within its global preoccupations. At the intergovernmental level, the central role has been taken over by the ILO, a specialised agency of the United Nations. The ILO cooperates with the United Nations and reports to its competent organs on major issues in the field of social policy. As already pointed out, one of its main preoccupations is the advancement of international social security law by means of conventions fixing objectives to be attained by members, or by means of agreements applicable to certain sectors of activity. Another major work assignment is technical assistance provided to developing countries in the introduction or improvement of social security schemes. Both programmes have considerable impact on the shape of social security schemes in different countries.

The standard-setting activities were originally developed as a means for encouraging industrialised countries to attain the most advanced levels of social security protection in the light of the available international experience. Following the massive affiliation of countries of the third world, this issue became problematic, as it was evident that the same standard could hardly be applicable to all. Consequently, it was the technical cooperation programme that became the chief instrument for the institutional advancement of social security in the developing world. But even this activity was not without its pitfalls. To prepare the launch of a social security scheme in a country, the ILO had to rely on national experts made available by different institutions; not all of them were capable, in addition to their technical skill, of mastering the delicate political aspects of the problem, which were, in the end, decisive. For this reason, many of the ILO reports remained in the drawers of national ministries without ever being acted upon. In more recent years, with most of the developing countries having established their schemes of social insurance, a new challenge has arisen for the ILO due to its involvement in United Nations programmes destined to reduce poverty. But this is a complex task, the implications of which have been discussed elsewhere in this study.

Many other intergovernmental organisations intervene in this field, such as the World Health Organization (WHO), on account of its involvement in medical care programmes, or the World Bank whose spectacular incursion in social security agenda at the international level has been discussed here at some length. The reports of the Organisation for Economic Co-operation and Development (OECD) have also left their mark on social security reforms in many countries through the impact they make on their economic establishment. And we have already mentioned the specific influence of regional organisations such as the EU. Although not competent to impose on its members a particular social security model, the EU has been known for putting considerable pressure on candidate countries prior to becoming members, consisting most of the time of a strong exhortation to reduce public expenditure on social security programmes.

Among the non-governmental bodies, a special mention has to be made of an organisation frequently referred to in this book, the International Social Security Association (ISSA). Founded in Brussels in October 1927, under the name of 'International Conference of National Unions of Mutual Benefit Societies and Sickness Insurance Funds', its object was to coordinate internationally and to intensify efforts for the development and improvement of sickness insurance, by the organisation of periodical meetings of members, by exchange of information and by comparison of experiences. Several motives were behind the creation of this body, the most immediate being the need felt by sickness insurance administrators to have their own international platform for the exchange of experience. They thus emerge as a new actor among those exercising an impact on the institution. It should be recalled that during the early years the Conference admitted to membership only self-administered funds and societies; the principle of self-administration was considered as the 'fundamental basis of its Constitution'. From the beginning, this initiative had the active support of the ILO, aware of the fact that no social legislation is of use if it cannot be properly administered; at the same time, the ILO leaders expected help at the national level with regard to ratifications of social insurance conventions. The promoters of the Conference sought in turn support from the ILO in defence of sickness insurance and its autonomous institutions, as well as material help regarding the activities of the secretariat. This mutual interest made it possible to launch the organisation only a few months after the adoption of the first ILO convention on sickness insurance.

This was until recently the full official explanation of motives behind the creation of the original institutional form of ISSA. An unofficial version circulating in ILO corridors contained an addendum suggesting that the real motive was the frustration of sickness insurance directors attending the conference only in an expert capacity and hence unable to take the floor and intervene in the discussions. In reality, the story is much more complex, as revealed by recent historical research (Guinand, 2008). The establishment of an international organisation of social insurance institutions was under discussion in various quarters from the mid-1920s. The first concrete step was made in 1926 when the director of sickness insurance of the Swiss canton of Basle contacted his colleagues in France and Germany with a view to convene in his hometown an international congress, which could possibly be used as a platform to launch a permanent international body. This initiative naturally met with the disapproval of ILO authorities; missions were immediately sent out to countries concerned so as to convince the competent leaders to block this move and adopt instead an ILO plan of action. This means that the crucial negotiations took place prior to the ILO conference in June 1927, which only provided the occasion to finalise the agreed arrangements.

Another important factor that moved the interested parties into swift action was the creation, in 1926, of an 'International Professional Association of Physicians', which was formally opposed to any form of compulsory sickness insurance. This was a significant threat to ILO social insurance policy and an obvious invitation to both compulsory sickness insurance funds as well as to mutual benefit societies to obtain their own international platform. The creation of an international sickness insurance body thus became a political necessity.

During the initial years of its existence, the activities of the Conference were practically limited to Europe – at the outbreak of the Second World War, Palestine and Peru were the only non-European countries represented. A major constitutional change took place in 1936, when, following the adoption of ILO conventions on invalidity, old-age and survivors' insurance, the organisation decided to cover these branches of social insurance and changed its name to 'International Social Insurance Conference' (better known under its French abbreviation of CIMAS). At this time, as pension institutions were often national in scope, with the state playing a major role in their administration, the requirement of self-administration was dropped from the qualifying conditions for membership. The sickness insurance funds had a stake in this development because during the period of economic crisis, old-age and invalidity insurance funds could take off their lists great many older and disabled unemployed people, claiming sickness benefits. As to the possible impact of the Conference on ratifications of ILO conventions, the overall judgement seems to be positive. During these years, the assemblies would pass resolutions demanding the maintenance of the level of benefits and insisting on the fact that the harder the pressure of the economic crisis, the greater was the need for social insurance. In the words of an international expert writing about this period: 'It is reasonable to believe that these resolutions had practical results, especially through their influence on parliaments' (ISSA, 1986, p 18). But as always in similar cases, it is difficult to produce evidence to this effect.

The activities of CIMAS were interrupted during the Second World War, when the ILO moved its headquarters to Montreal. On return to Geneva, the competent international circles hotly debated the proposal of the French government to create a special United Nations agency to deal with social security. But a vast majority preferred to maintain this competence within the ILO and to adapt CIMAS to the new world of social security administration. A General Assembly convened in Geneva in 1947 gave the organisation a new name and a new constitution, also admitting the membership of those government departments directly responsible for the management of at least one branch of social security. By that time, some of the autonomous institutions that were among the founders of the organisation in the late 1920s disappeared to make way for state administrations, while others were sitting there side by side with the government departments of other countries, including those of the US, USSR, Great Britain, Canada and others. ISSA, which technically remained a non-governmental organisation, thus became an international body *sui generis*; it succeeded in maintaining an independent, non-bureaucratic approach to problems of social security, greatly helped by the persisting cooperative spirit of its members.

Throughout the first decades of the post-war period, ISSA witnessed a tremendous increase in membership. While in 1947 it could count 39 members in 21 countries (15 in Europe, five in America and one in Asia), by the time of its 60th anniversary in 1987, it represented 252 members in 114 countries (29 in Europe, 35 in Africa, 31 in America and 19 in Asia). ISSA was still chiefly concerned with the administrative aspects of social security but its programme had to be adapted to the needs of its members. While several Permanent Committees, established for each risk or specific aspect of management, followed the most progressive developments worldwide, regional activities catered for the needs of its members at the level proper to each region. Finally, as discussed earlier, research activities were developed mainly for the benefit of membership in industrialised countries. ISSA was thus complementing the work of the ILO at the intergovernmental level and provided general support for the effort aimed at the promotion of the institution and the improvement of its operations. It will be of interest to note that within the framework of actions undertaken on the occasion of its 60th anniversary, the ISSA Secretariat ran a survey among the member organisations, attempting to elicit information on concrete instances when legislative or administrative improvements were obtained as a direct result of participation in ISSA activities. In a few cases only could the officials of the replying institution point to an innovation introduced at the national level, following information obtained through technical reports, publications, or personal contacts made on the occasion of meetings. But they all agreed that the overall impact was positive, ISSA providing the necessary general background knowledge for all institutional advancement. This enquiry also confirmed the view held by many, that the beneficial effect of an international organisation consisted not only in the quality of its technical work, but also – if not chiefly – in the very fact of bringing together people with similar interests and missions.

The general orientation and content of ISSA's work started changing in the closing decade of the 20th century due to economic pressure and the need for rationalisation of all activities, and also to gradually changing priorities in the social protection field at the global level. The division of responsibilities between the ILO and ISSA, dictated by the situation in the formative years, ceased to make sense. The international conventions could no longer be considered the main raison d'être of the ILO, while the protection against the encroachment of governmental power over the self-managed institutions had ceased to be of interest to ISSA even before the Second World War. In the social protection sector, increasing economic difficulties often bring about a move towards a stronger government control or even a take-over of administrative responsibilities. This was gradually reflected in the growth of the governmental element in ISSA membership. As result, the artificial division between social policy questions being reserved for the ILO and questions of administrative implementation belonging to ISSA lost its meaning.

This point is well illustrated by the change in the content of the main ISSA publication, the quarterly *International Social Security Review*. An analysis of the institutional background of authors of articles published in the review reveals that if in the 1980s the vast majority came from social security institutions, in the 1990s the majority belonged to academic research. In this way, the review, which used to be a monitor of the organisational life of ISSA as well as a platform for publication of general studies on social security, became exclusively a research publication. This means that ISSA has acquired a platform from which to influence the formation of social policy, independently of its legal status of a non-governmental organisation.

The wind of change has blown also in the ILO's approach to the modalities of this mutual collaboration. The economic crisis and the retrenchment of the welfare state reduced the political importance of the ILO in the United Nations family and gave a dominating position to the World Bank. The latter's attack against social security in the closing decade of the 20th century led to the creation of a common front, with ISSA providing a solid basis for the necessary defensive action. And its robust presence may have constituted an invitation to the ILO to reduce the level of its engagement in the classical field of social insurance and to pay more attention to the problems of the developing world. This did not fail in turn to cause an uneasy feeling among ISSA members, who knew perfectly well that in many respects the ILO action was irreplaceable. Even if ISSA today has the position and means to influence a great number of actors playing an important role in the institutional development of social security, and even if it can master the social policy issues as well as the practical implementation of the corresponding legislation, it does has not have the capacity to replace the ILO in its role as the specialised United Nations agency responsible for the social protection sector.

The impact of the two organisations is complementary and vigorous action on both sides is needed to preserve the future development of the institution.

## Note

[1] A well-known French authority on the subject, Alfred Sauvy of *Collège de France*, presented a paper on social security and demography.

# SIX

# The use of macro-sociological factor analysis in comparative studies

As mentioned in the previous chapter, this factor analysis, submitted for consideration to ISSA research bodies, was intended from the very beginning to serve as a tool for comparative studies. The idea was to accompany a descriptive presentation of a social security scheme with a brief survey of macro-sociological factors at work behind its creation and evolution, so as to make this 'dynamic picture' of the institution the object of comparison. The advantage of this approach was a better understanding of the significance, structure and functional operations of each scheme within its societal environment and hence a more precise comparative analysis. What was missing, however, was the capacity to measure the end product of the whole institutional machinery, in line with the ambitions of social engineering current at that time.

## Comparing the social product of the institution

In a paper presented to the first Round Table Meeting on the Sociology of Social Security held in September 1966 in Evian (Rys, 1966), the suggestion was made to complete the macro-sociological factor analysis with a second stage of the study, whereby the working results of the institution would be compared against the social policy objectives of the government concerned and against the standards set up by the existing international law. In this way, and with the use of appropriate indices, the study was to reveal specific trends in the evolution of the institution at the international level.

The plan for this second stage was based on the assumption that in order to ensure comparability, the study should be limited to social insurance only. The working of the scheme should be described in terms of contingencies and groups of beneficiaries covered, and of financial techniques used; further analysis would be devoted to institutional structures and finally to the social product. This latter concept raised the question of how to measure the tangible results of social security operations consisting of income transfers and services in favour of specific population groups. It was clear from the beginning that expenditure on benefits in cash and in kind was not an absolute indicator; to obtain more significant information, it was necessary to ask questions, such as:

- Are the benefits reaching the appropriate categories?
- Are the entitled persons really in need of the benefit?
- Do the benefits reach them in time?

The conclusion was that the real measure of social product was not expenditure, but the efficiency in meeting the social need the benefit was supposed to meet. With this reflection, however, the project opened some highly controversial issues, highlighted in the round table meeting discussions.[1]

The principal objection was that the proposal to conduct studies relating the working results of a social security scheme to the objectives envisaged in the basic legislation assumed the existence of a coherent social security policy. In reality, however, national social security schemes were anything but coherent, owing to the particular nature of their development. Internal incoherence, which is of political origin, eventually becomes institutional in so far as it reflects different preoccupations of the legislator at different points of time. In order to be able to carry out the studies proposed in the paper, it would therefore be necessary to study first 'the dialectics of the evolution of national systems and their internal inconsistencies' (ISSA, 1966, p 236). This, admittedly, was a task beyond the scope of a normal comparative study.

## Taking account of the 'cultural factor'

Another major issue in the discussion was the pertinence of a simultaneous study of what was referred to as the 'cultural factor'. It was pointed out that in certain countries it was this factor more than the material situation of society that determined the shape of the national social security system. The suggestion was made that to the extent that some of the most acute problems of social security development are encountered at the cultural level, sociologists should pay as much attention to them as to those of the demographic or economic order.

The editorial comment on the cultural factor raises the question of how it can be defined, analysed and eventually also compared. It suggests that in the end it is 'the sum total of the experience in social welfare which a society has acquired and expressed in institutionalised or other forms of behaviour and in the attitudes of its members' (ISSA, 1966, p 239). In this way the study of the cultural factor is identified with a general historical study of social security and of its institutional predecessors within the respective societal environment. It is only when the social institution is historically understood and its significance explained that a meaningful sociological factor analysis may take place.

The Evian round table meeting had broadly agreed that there was a need for sociologists to concentrate their attention on comparative studies, as suggested in the introductory paper. In the subsequent years, however, the proposed blueprint for macro-sociological factor analysis was not followed in any significant way. The reasons for it are discussed in more detail later. Nevertheless, the emphasis placed on a multidisciplinary approach made an impact on subsequent developments of social research in this field.

## The question of practical applicability

The search for an optimum understanding of the significance, structure and functional operations of social security has led to the elaboration of a very demanding method of work. The researcher is expected to master in each case the history of a scheme before proceeding to a more detailed analysis in the light of the information on its societal environment, provided by four social sciences most directly concerned with it. This in itself is a challenge because not all of the required knowledge is readily available and may call for a certain amount of ad hoc research work or collection of data. The difficulties involved in this undertaking have been well highlighted by Else Oyen, already cited in our historical note on the sociology of social security: 'The system of social security is difficult to penetrate for outsiders in any country.... It takes years to understand the system well enough to make it an object of research' (Oyen, 1986, p 219).

Clearly, there are no hard rules to determine at which point a researcher is ready to undertake a comparative study, but the basic requirements alone limit the number of potential candidates. Even when comparing countries using the same language, such as Austria and Germany, or the US and the UK, care has to be taken to learn the technical terminology specific to each country in order to avoid misinterpretations. When comparing across the language barriers, it is important that the researcher has at least a basic knowledge of the languages used so as to be able go to the original sources. Translated material prepared for different purposes is not always reliable. And most importantly, experience has shown that it is not enough to have an expert knowledge of the situation in one country to be potentially equipped for comparative work. In fact, this may become a negative factor in that it may lead to a certain mental blockage and incapacity to open one's mind to different concepts and approaches. The most important requirement for a comparative researcher thus seems to be a capacity for 'transcultural thinking', requiring a certain amount of intuitive understanding of social problems within society. It is no doubt for this reason that comparative studies have sometimes been considered as a kind of art, rather than a strict scientific discipline (Higgins, 1981, p 7).

Another difficulty is linked to the lack of basic theoretical models indispensable for the formulation of generally valid conclusions. Comparing the organisation and functions of social security institutions in two countries may be in itself an interesting and instructive exercise, but it cannot lead to any general conclusions unless their respective situations are seen in relation to a certain abstract model, representing a standard image of the institution at the international level. Consequently, it is not so much the similarities and divergences between the two institutions under study that are of interest, but rather the relationship of each of them to the above abstract model. The construction or even the awareness of the existence of such a model is obviously not easy to obtain and seems to be the result of accumulated personal knowledge and lengthy experience of working in the sector, rather than the result of some specific conceptual effort.

All this raises the question of whether the proposed blueprint is viable and practically applicable. The reply is affirmative, provided that a certain number of rules are observed. It follows from what we have said before that any purely quantitative, statistical or descriptive treatment of data is to be excluded. Since the basic requirement is the explanation of the social significance of each scheme within the given society, the use of a qualitative exploratory approach is indispensable. But this may take place at different levels according to the availability of data. Not every comparative study applying this method should require lengthy historical in-depth investigation, followed by a detailed analysis of the demographic, economic, sociological and political factors. In some cases a selective approach to relevant data may produce satisfactory results.

## The use of macro-sociological factor analysis in more recent studies

In an attempt to develop a 'short-cut version' of this method I have tried to analyse the interaction of macro-sociological factors to explain differences in the evolution of social security reform in transition countries of Central Europe (Rys, 2002). While broadly confirming the predominance of the political factor in the reform process in the three selected countries (Czech Republic, Hungary and Poland), the study nevertheless demonstrated that in certain circumstances the economic factor, jointly with one or another of the external factors, may play a more decisive role. In more concrete terms, and with a special reference to the pension sector, the situation may be summed up as follows:

- Social security reform in the Czech Republic had followed fairly closely the development of the political situation in the country. In the absence of any major economic crisis, the outcome of the reform was the result of a compromise between the major political forces, negotiated under a right-wing coalition government led by a neoliberal party. The reform adapted the existing pension system to the conditions of the market economy but rejected any partial privatisation of the state scheme. A relatively low level of foreign debt reduced the influence of external factors, particularly that of the World Bank.
- The situation was quite different in Hungary where, in 1994, a socialist-led left-of-centre coalition replaced a right-wing government. This tried at first to reconcile capitalism with the 'social advantages' of the previous regime but failed to find the necessary financial resources. The result was a drastic 'reform package' in 1995, subsequently suspended in most of its provisions by the Constitutional Tribunal. Nevertheless, this government succeeded, before the end of its mandate, to introduce, in 1997, a pension reform based on the three-pillar system proposed by the World Bank. This history demonstrates the overriding power of the economic factor when financial resources for social policy enjoying political preference in parliament are entirely lacking. However, the political factor regains its importance as soon as the state of economic emergency disappears.
- In the Polish case, the political factor governed the evolution of the reform during the whole preparatory period, although the economic situation was very serious. Four general elections took place during that time, giving the country governments of different political colour. After a long legislative standstill, a pension reform plan was agreed by a majority opinion across the spectrum of political parties before its adoption in 1999. This reform, also based on the World Bank model, went even further in the transformation of the system than in Hungary. In this country the political decision was taken under the combined pressure of the demographic and economic

factors, in the presence of a strong external pressure exercised by the World Bank.

Other authors have used a similar approach in an effort to obtain more refined analytical tools for the study of the economic and political environment of social security. Thus, for instance, Katharina Müller (2001), in her analysis of the determinants of the Czech, Hungarian and Polish pension reform, examines the position of several corporative actors within and outside the government and their perception of available choices in the context of existing structural and institutional factors. The actors include, at the governmental level, Ministries of Social Affairs, Ministries of Finance and the World Bank, while the non-governmental actors are trades unions, employers' confederations and associations of retired persons. Among the main structural factors are the volume of foreign debt of the country and the financial situation of competent social security institutions. One of the major questions raised in the study is why Hungary and Poland went ahead with a partial privatisation of their pension systems while the Czech Republic held it back. In her conclusions, the author explains that a radical pension reform becomes feasible when those actors advocating pension privatisation – that is, the Ministry of Finance and the World Bank – have stakes and leverage in the reform process; privatisation is not likely to take place when the only governmental actor involved is the Ministry of Social Affairs, responsible for the policy and administrative supervision of the existing social insurance scheme. [2]

Pension reform in post-communist countries was the subject of another study, which concentrated its attention on the analysis of political and structural factors. In addition to Hungary and Poland, Mitchell Orenstein (2000) enlarged his geographic basis to cover Kazakhstan, to study in some detail the deliberative process leading to the adoption of a reform. As distinct from the analysis of actors used by Müller, he differentiates between *institutional veto and proposal actors* (governments, Ministries of Finance, Ministries of Social Affairs), *partisan actors* (political parties) and *interest groups* (both state and civil society organisations, such as social security institutions, trades unions, pensioners' associations and private pension funds). His principal finding confirms a fairly commonsense observation that countries with a large number of actors intervening in the reform process (Hungary and Poland) will adopt a less radical reform than a country with a less representative political system (Kazakhstan). The author also observes that while the consensus-finding process in countries with a plurality of actors takes much longer, the subsequent acceptance of new measures and public participation are much easier to obtain.

It is probably not without reason that these three studies have chosen to deal with societies that faced the problems of reorganisation of social security after the upheavals caused by the fall of communism. A macro-sociological approach to the study of the institution is particularly rewarding when the main forces of the societal environment are in movement and can be more easily observed. At the present time, globalisation is one such current affecting all countries of the world and highlights the need for a deeper analysis of what we have referred to here as external factors that shape social security policies. A recent example of this interest is the initiative of the Network for European Social Policy Analysis (ESPAnet), which in Helsinki in September 2008 convened a conference addressing 'cross-border influences in social policy'.

While lacking the conceptual facility and convenience of the classification of social security schemes into preconceived categories – which carries a certain risk of the deformation of social reality – it seems that macro-sociological factor analysis will remain an indispensable tool of study, particularly in situations when an institution is exposed to major changes in its societal environment. This is certainly the case at present and it is to be hoped that an appropriate deep analysis of political, economic, social and demographic factors will accompany any future reforms.

## Note

[1] A summary of the discussions of this meeting as well as the main papers are reproduced in a special issue of the *Bulletin of the ISSA*, 1966, vol 19, nos 7-8.

[2] While the study itself is very pertinent, this particular conclusion was later questioned by Czech experts who pointed out that the main reason for the position of the Czech government was political rather than economic. With an eye on the forthcoming general elections, the neoliberal Prime Minister Klaus did not even dare to formulate a proposal with a view to reducing the scope of the general pension system.

# Part Three

Reinventing social security in times of economic crisis: foundations of a new political consensus

# SEVEN

# Adapting social security to a new societal environment

It would be hardly feasible to attempt in this book and at this point in time a regular macro-sociological factor analysis of the position of social security institutions in times of economic crisis. But the previous chapters have given us the necessary parameters so as to be able to formulate a judgement on which to base our search for possible ways of preserving the institution from a lasting deterioration and progressive dismantlement.

## The impact of economic crises on the institution in a historical perspective

The essential problem of all social security measures based on social insurance has been known from the very beginning, and particularly from the time of the economic crisis in the early 1930s – the simultaneous impact of a reduction in revenue due to a shortfall of contributions paid by a shrinking labour force and defaulting enterprises, and of an increase in expenditure on unemployment benefits with a collateral rise in the volume of long-term sickness, disability and old-age pension benefits. With respect to the last-mentioned risks, experience has shown that during a period of mass unemployment there is an obvious tendency on the part of those who for some reason are not eligible for unemployment benefit to have recourse to the corresponding branches of social insurance.

The numerous and varied reactions to this dramatic situation may have both positive and negative aspects. On the positive side is the resulting pressure on public authorities to take steps towards the improvement of existing social security coverage, as we saw in the impetus given to the development of old-age and disability insurance during the period between the First and Second World Wars. The obvious danger is the tendency of public authorities to use and abuse social security institutions and benefits they provide as the main line of defence or even remedy against what is essentially an economic disease of society. This was the case of the mistaken policy practised in some countries during the period after the first oil shock in the

1970s, which threatened to ruin all branches of social insurance affected by mass unemployment. Fortunately, the message that remedies against unemployment have to be found in measures dealing with the promotion of employment rather than in social security benefits was received before it was too late.

There is no doubt that throughout the past history of social security the main solution to problems caused by the impact of an economic crisis came from the change in the economic environment itself and from the return to some kind of prosperity. Admittedly, the institution suffered and did not quite recover its previous social effectiveness, but that was considered acceptable in view of the changed societal environment. There are indications that many people today look forward to seeing history repeat itself and hope for a prompt economic recovery. But is this the only reasonable thing to do – is there not another way of improving the situation and make the institution more resistant to periodic onslaughts of economic upheavals? The answer to this question is worthy of some investigation.

The most immediate approach that comes to mind would be to increase the level of contributions of those remaining in the labour force and reduce the level of benefits paid so as to help preserve the financial equilibrium of the institution. But this is hardly conceivable given its ultimate purpose, which is to help people to overcome crisis situations in life; reducing benefits at a time when they are most needed cannot serve this purpose.

In the original concept of its founders, social security was never meant to serve as a weapon to combat the economic evils of society. As mentioned earlier, Beveridge himself pointed out that social security was meant to deal with risks to which an individual remains exposed even when the conditions of society as a whole are as good as they can be, and specifically excluded from its definition measures aimed at improving the general conditions of society such as those regarding employment. Accordingly, if social security is to be preserved to deal with physiological and social risks generated by society in 'normal' conditions, any dysfunction of the economic system, such as mass unemployment, should be dealt with by economic measures. Social security institutions should hence receive special help from funds provided by the economic system of each country should they be called upon to maintain their benefits in such an exceptional situation.

## The initial impact of the present economic crisis

Before moving on to develop this argument, let us have a look at the magnitude of the threat that the present economic conditions of society represent for social security institutions worldwide. At the time of writing, we have at our disposal the results of a survey carried out by ISSA among its member organisations between February and April 2009 (ISSA, 2009). Responses to the survey were received from 47 social security institutions from all regions of the world covering among them tens of millions of people for all major branches of social insurance. The questionnaire sought information about the overall impact of the global economic crisis, the impact on pension and unemployment programmes, as well as the policy responses that have been adopted to reduce the social impacts and to restore confidence in the institution.

The overall results indicate that it is still too early to measure the full social impact of the crisis. Nevertheless, the classical reactions of social security systems are already apparent. The crisis has caused significant losses in investments of social security funds, particularly those in industrialised countries, some of them reporting the loss of as much as five years of investment income and around 25% of the net asset value of the fund. These results indicate that the crisis will challenge the financial viability of all schemes that rely on funding. The second classical phenomenon is less income due to fewer contributors and higher expenses due to additional beneficiaries.

The decline of revenues is caused not only by a reduction in the number of contributors and a loss of income from investments but also by lower government subsidies and cross-subsidies between schemes, as well as by an increase of non-compliance by covered enterprises. Measures such as stopping the scheduled increase in rates of contributions, or reducing current rates, may in the short term increase the disposable income of an enterprise but may lead to a financial imbalance of social security institutions. Similarly, the increase in the volume of benefits is due not only to a higher number of beneficiaries as result of mass unemployment but also to the pressure put on the institutions to mitigate the impact of the crisis on people through the provision of additional social security and social assistance benefits to protect the most vulnerable. The member organisations also report that governments that have provided assistance to financial institutions and adopted economic recovery measures have also generally included assistance to social security agencies.

With regard to the performance of social security funds, interestingly enough, social security institutions in developing countries show better results than those in industrialised countries. This may be attributed to the fact that their funds generally cannot invest abroad, the investments are made mainly in fixed income assets, or their markets have not been seriously impacted by the crisis.

Obviously, this is only a preliminary account of the difficulties that lie ahead. It is usually in the second year following the onset of an economic crisis that serious problems start to threaten the survival of the institution.

## National economy as a permanent support of social security systems

Since the cause of the present upheaval is a dysfunction in the prevailing world economic order, it would seem natural that the necessary preventive mechanism should be established and possible remedies found within each national economy. The idea of looking for links with the national economy and taking account of the evolution of the economic situation in the calculation of social security contributions and benefits is not new. The most serious attempt towards providing this link has been made in the pension legislation of Sweden, elaborated during the last decade of the 20th century, which came fully into force in 2003.

The Swedish pension system contains a basic minimum pension for all residents guaranteed by the state and an earnings-related scheme that consists of two parts: a fully funded premium reserve scheme financed by a contribution amounting to 2.5% of covered earnings and a pay-as-you-go scheme based on a notional defined contribution plan financed by a contribution representing 16% of earnings.[1]

The part that is of interest to us is the pay-as-you-go scheme with benefit indexation rules linked to average wages and life expectancy. This system contains two important features. The first is an *automatic balancing mechanism*, which makes it possible to estimate the current assets and liabilities of the scheme. If the estimated liabilities of the scheme exceed its assets, the yearly revaluation of pension rights and pensions in payment will be based not on average earnings but on a value that enables pension liabilities to grow at the same rate as the system's assets. This means that whatever happens, the balancing mechanism reduces the current and future pensions as much as is needed in order to restore financial equilibrium. But it also means – as Scherman (2005, p 114) rightly points out – that while this mechanism guarantees the financial stability of the pay-as-you-go system, it does not guarantee adequate pensions.

It is, however, the second special feature that is of most direct interest to our present reflections. This is the creation of a *buffer fund*, the purpose of which is to prevent every change in the ratio between the numbers of active and retired persons directly transforming into a change of the value of pensions in payment. Since the system is using as a rule the indexation on average earnings, the buffer fund will grow with an increase of labour participation and diminish in times of high unemployment. The surpluses of the fund are used to reduce financial strains on the systems at such a time.[2] It is in fact this financial reserve that guarantees that people receive adequate pensions.

No information is available at the time of writing about the performance of the above-described mechanism faced with the consequences of the present economic crisis. However, to the extent that it has been designed to deal with current variations in standard factors used for the calculation of pension benefits, it is most unlikely that it could deal with drastic modifications of the labour market due to the dysfunctions of the present economic system. But this is not fundamental for our present reflections. What counts is the idea of building up reserves in times of plenty for use in times of difficulties.

As mentioned earlier, social security institutions have not been designed for and should not be used as the chief weapon to deal with the consequences of defaults inherent in an existing economic system. If they are to fulfil the role that is essential for the preservation of the existing world order, their economic sustainability should be ensured by the constitution of reserve funds to be used in periods of economic crises and for the dysfunctions of the prevailing economic system. These funds should be entirely independent from regular social security financing and should be provided directly by the economy. Taking account of the current public discussion concerning the causes of the virtual collapse of the financial system, it should not be forbidden to think in terms of possible levies on excessive salaries of leaders of financial institutions or any other type of excessive remuneration of an economic activity. This could also cover levies on proceeds of speculative investments that, as much as excessive salaries, contribute to the creation of periodic crises in an economic system.

## Search for a new political consensus on social security

Confidence in the existing social security systems based on the transparency of their operations is the key line describing the basis on which to build a new political consensus regarding the institution. This is featured in the recommendations of the EU, as much as in the most recent declarations of ISSA concerning the economic crisis. Thus, for instance, in a report on the coordination of pension policies adopted by the European Council in March 2003, one of the objectives states that governments should strive to 'make pension systems more transparent and adaptable to changing circumstances, so that citizens can continue to have confidence in them...' (Scherman, 2005, p 115). The earlier-mentioned ISSA survey on social security in times of crisis openly calls for policy responses 'to restore confidence in public social security programmes' (ISSA, 2009, p 1).

The loss of confidence in existing social security schemes hence seems to be considered as an established fact. The reasons are obvious – the present financial and economic crisis came after a period of reforms with the objective of alleviating the financial burden on the state and transferring it to occupational and private arrangements, particularly in the pension field. Ingenious policy inventions such as the notional defined contribution plan have helped to pave the way for a general transition from defined benefit to defined contribution systems without any protest from the insured population who generally believe that their future social income may benefit from a direct exposure to commercial markets. The tremendous losses suffered by the pension funds since the middle of 2008 marked the minds not only of people of pensionable age and those in sight of it but also the mentality of younger generations who seem to be losing faith in the assurance of a comfortable income in old age. This lack of confidence will obviously have a major impact on the political support social security needs in all societies at all times in order to achieve its objectives.

In order to regain the lost confidence of the public, the social security schemes of the future will have to be perfectly transparent in their operations, indicating to every insured person the cost of their total contribution effort and the benefit obtained. This means, in more concrete terms of the above-quoted EU pension objective, that governments must:

> develop reliable and easy-to-understand information on
> the long-term perspectives of pension systems, notably

with regard to the likely evolution of benefit levels and contribution rates, to promote the broadest possible consensus regarding pension policies and reforms and to improve the methodological basis for efficient monitoring of pension reforms and policies. (Scherman, 2005, p 115)

The notion of transparency would also require a periodic individual report to every insured person indicating the amount of the benefit that can be envisaged under different scenarios. Social security experts are aware that many people have great difficulties in making comparisons between amounts based on the present value of money and real wage levels and future projections based on different assumptions; this situation is not made any easier by a general tendency on the part of competent institutions to present information about future developments in a more optimistic way than may be warranted. It is particularly at this point that it becomes clear that more and better social security requires more and better citizen education.

In present-day society, transparency is a condition sine qua non for the achievement of a basic political consensus on social security policy. If in previous centuries, calculations and projections of social security actuaries could have had something mysterious about them, present generations wish to know the facts, especially when it is a question of their own well-being. And as any person with some experience in comparative studies will note, agreements on social policy are easier to reach if people on both sides of the table know their facts. No doubt ideologies still determine people's basic attitudes towards social questions, but at the same time, there has been a noticeable trend to reduce their impact in search of a better factual knowledge about life and people. It may hence be necessary to restrain still further some idealist beliefs about what should be, in favour of a better recognition of what is.

Contrary to the conviction of many sincere believers in the virtue of vigorous income redistribution through social security under the banner of overall citizen solidarity, it may be more appropriate to search for references closer to real human nature and favour that type of solidarity, which makes sense also from the point of view of self-interest. This should aim at bringing the level of income redistribution through social security up to that point where, it can be reasonably argued, an individual needs social protection so as to obtain cover against those risks that personal resources and private insurance normally cannot guarantee. This in fact is the very essence of social insurance and even if the breaking point between the 'self-interest' contribution and 'solidarity' contribution may vary from one individual to another, a broad political consensus on the question should be attainable.

Such policy would have the advantage of liberating social security operations from any suspicion of a politically biased measure, since the majority supporting the agreed level of contributions and hence the agreed level of income redistribution would cut across all political parties. This consensus could thus usefully replace the losing appeal of the left-wing political parties to a citizen solidarity seriously damaged by the collective experience under the communist regime. In this perspective, the requirement of transparency regarding the income-redistribution impact of social security operations would become for governments the question of basic honesty towards their citizens.

**Notes**

[1] For a full description of the Swedish system, see Scherman (2005).

[2] It should be pointed out that at the time of the Swedish reform a pension reserve fund equivalent to five and a half years of total pension payments was already available.

# Final reflections

In this book I have tried to draw a lesson from a lifelong observation of the working of social security with a view to identifying a certain number of fundamentals that are highlighted by its historical evolution. If a sustainable development of social security is the goal, these fundamentals should be respected so as to preserve the institution for future generations.

But what institution do we want, or, more precisely, what institution is likely to survive in view of the deep economic crisis of the present time? A brief overview of the history that was presented in the opening pages of this book shows the variety of replies that people have given at different stages of societal development to the question of how to ensure some degree of material security for individual existence in society. The permanent leitmotiv of this evolution is a search for an ever-wider collective basis for a suitable institutional arrangement, from the mutual help within an occupational group to the overgrown social protection infrastructure of the communist state.

Unfortunately, we have learned – and paid a high price for this lesson – that the communist model of social comfort does not work in the long run, partly because it costs more than this type of collectivist society can afford, taking into account the fact that at the same time it reduces its productive capacity. More importantly, the communist state imposes a trade-off between the guaranteed social protection system and political freedom; experience has shown that for most people political freedom represents a higher degree of security of social and individual existence. The extreme end of the evolutionary cycle of the collectivist provision of social security is hence not what our contemporary vocabulary would call a 'good practice', and we have to look elsewhere for a better solution.

The macro-sociological studies of social security that were reviewed in Part Two of this book highlight the overriding importance of the political factor in the evolution of the institution, which is taking place within the limits dictated by the economic situation of society and under the influence of a number of other societal factors directly intervening in this process. Consequently, if the institution is to be assured of a long-term development, it has to be politically acceptable to a wide spectre of existing parties and ideologies, and affordable under the prevailing conditions of the national economy. Both political acceptability and economic sustainability can be greatly enhanced by a system that uses an understandable and transparent method of income transfers within a system based on social insurance.

The notion of political acceptability is directly dependent on economic sustainability. As long as the capitalist market economy remains the world-dominating order, the cost of the social security system falling on the enterprise will have to stay within reasonable limits so as not to hinder free competition in production and trade. It is unlikely that a political majority in a country could adopt a different policy on a long-term basis. But there is also the question of the economic burden falling on the individual. Over the years and for a number of reasons, the readiness of the middle classes to assume a generous measure of redistribution of income in favour of economically weaker citizens has considerably eroded. The cost of provisions against social risks is constantly growing and increasing longevity is accelerating the trend. The improved standard of living of the majority of the population weakens the need for the maintenance of a high-level safety net, while the call for the satisfaction of the basic necessities of the poor through social aid is getting a more favourable reception. It would hence make sense to reduce the charge on the middle-class wage-earner by reducing the redistributive function of social security to an acceptable level.

This reduction has to be accompanied by full transparency of charges and benefits for the individual resulting from income transfers operated by social insurance schemes. Nearly a century ago, during a discussion on the introduction of National Insurance in 1911, a young British politician, Winston S. Churchill, spoke warmly about 'bringing in the magic of averages to the rescue of the millions' (Bruce, 1961, p 168). Over the years, the social insurance magic has lost its attraction in the process of large-scale redistribution of income among social classes. The citizen of the 21st century will want to know precisely who is paying what into the system and who is getting what out of it. In other words, they will want full transparency of the impact of financial flows of social insurance – which should not create problems in our advanced computer age.

But economic adequacy and redistributive transparency are not the only aspects of political acceptability. The history of social security is directly linked to the idea of social justice. The principle of social insurance appeals partly to the rational self-interest of the individual, assuring them of access to benefits not normally attainable through private means, but also partly to their natural sentiment of solidarity and respect for other human beings. When it comes to the essentials of social security, it is not just any scheme of income transfers that makes the institution what it is. It is only that scheme, which guarantees dignity to beneficiaries by granting benefits as of right – the result of their status as active participants and contributors to the scheme. Some may consider this insistence somewhat old-fashioned taking account of the development of mentalities in younger generations. But let there be no mistake – most conflicts in the present troubled world start with the question of offended human dignity, in the absence of generally accepted rules and norms of behaviour. Respecting individual integrity and human dignity contributes to maintaining social peace within nations, as much as an active pursuit of social justice and democratic ways of running society.

Regarding the question of recent trends in the global development of social security, under the impact of recurrent financial crises and the growth of poverty, many governments both in the industrialised and developing countries seek a solution to specific social problems in new measures combining a social insurance approach with that of social aid. And since under certain circumstances it is easier to obtain the necessary financial resources from ad hoc taxes or the state budget than through social insurance contributions, that practice becomes more widespread. This development is unhealthy because it leads to a progressive blurring of frontiers between two different systems and approaches, which in the long run can only result in the erosion of social insurance principles and a general recourse to state-financed social assistance methods.

It is possible that, under the influence of generally short-term economic thinking, many people no longer see the difference between social insurance benefits and those paid under state-financed social aid measures, as long as some financial help is forthcoming. It is this lack of sensibility of purely economic criteria to questions relating to the individual human perception of benefits and their social significance, which contributes to this trend. If this attitude becomes a general rule, we shall soon hear the argument that social insurance lacks flexibility and prevents the short-term transfer of funds to critical social areas according to the needs of the economic system. When this view carries the day, it will not take long to dismantle the institution of social insurance, in line with the ideology that has always considered it an unwelcome cancerous growth in the body of the capitalist system of the economy.

There remains the question of changing attitudes and reactions of new generations to the return of social insecurity. The founder of the French social security system, Pierre Laroque, once made the following observation:

> There is in every human being an inherent need of security. In all continents at all times, in all civilisations and cultures, people feared the uncertainty of days to come. If for some persons such uncertainty may constitute a stimulating challenge, for the vast majority of men and women it is a source of paralysing anxiety. (MIRE-ISSA, 1991, p 15)

In the past, books have been written on the subject of social security stifling the spirit of initiative and enterprise. However, Laroque's assessment of the situation seems to be nearer to the truth. For this reason, the policy of helping the strong at the expense of the weaker members of society is unlikely to become a trademark of a truly democratic government.

There are some indications that, faced with the present decline of social security provisions in many countries, young people are beginning to realise the precarious nature of the social benefits that they may expect to receive as time goes by. It seems that the general reaction is to take advantage of alternative forms of welfare, if available and accessible. But there is another reaction that may prevail should such alternative provisions prove to be beyond the reach of the majority. This would undoubtedly take the form of a global rejection of the existing social order and its replacement with a totalitarian collectivist regime of the kind the world has known in the not so distant past.

The last century marked considerable progress in the formulation of human rights and freedom guaranties. But human rights may constitute a dangerous illusion unless accompanied by material conditions for safeguarding them, and personal freedom may have little meaning if it is reduced to a permanent struggle for survival. We have insisted on several occasions in this book that the existing capitalist system of the market economy did not win its ideological struggle against communism in the closing decades of the last century. In fact – and the present world economic crisis provides the best evidence to this effect – thus far it has not given any convincing proof of its own long-term sustainability. To be able to do so, the reinstatement of social security into all of its basic functions and the constitution of appropriate financial reserves ensuring its operations during periods of economic difficulties would seem to be of vital importance. What is required is not just a parametric adjustment of the existing social insurance schemes, but a fundamental change in the general approach to the coordination of social and economic policies.

# References

Aaron, H. (1963) 'Social security in an expanding economy', Doctoral dissertation, Harvard University.

Abel-Smith, B. (1992) 'The Beveridge Report: its origins and outcomes', in *Social Security 50 Years after Beveridge*, Plenary papers of an International Conference held at University of York, England.

Adler, M., Bell, C., Clasen, J. and Sinfield, A. (eds) (1991) *The Sociology of Social Security*, Edinburgh: Edinburgh University Press.

Baldwin, P. (1990) *The Politics of Social Solidarity: Class Bases of the European Welfare State 1875 – 1975*, Cambridge: Cambridge University Press.

Baldwin, P. (1992) 'Beveridge in the Longue Duree', in *Social Security 50 Years after Beveridge*, Plenary papers of an International Conference held at University of York, England.

Barr, N. (2000) *Reforming Pensions: Myths, Truths and Policy Choices*, Working Paper 139, Washington, DC: IMF.

Barrientos, A. (2007) 'The role of tax-financed social security', *International Social Security Review*, vol 60, nos 2-3, pp 99-117.

Berra, J. (2000) *La structure des systèmes de sécurité sociale: Etude de droit comparé*, Lausanne: IRAL.

Beveridge, J. (1954) *Beveridge and his Plan*, London: Hodder and Stoughton.

Beveridge, W. (1942) *Social Insurance and Allied Services*, Cmd 6404, London: HMSO.

Booth, C. (1903) *Survey of London Life and Labour*, London: Macmillan.

Bridgen, P. and Meyer, T. (2005) 'When do benevolent capitalists change their mind? Explaining the retrenchment of defined-benefit pensions in Britain', *Social Policy and Administration*, vol 39, no 7, pp 764-85.

Bruce, M. (1961) *The Coming of the Welfare State*, London: Batsford.

Castles, F.G. (2004) *The Future of the Welfare State: Crisis Myths and Crisis Realities*, Oxford: Oxford University Press.

Churchill, W.S. (1909) *Liberalism and the Social Problem*, London: Hodder and Stoughton.

Cichon, M. and Hagemejer, K. (2007) 'Changing the development policy paradigm: investing in a social security floor for all', *International Social Security Review*, vol 60, nos 2-3, pp 169-96.

Clotuche, G. (2005) 'Réformes de la protection sociale et l'UE', dans *Efficience des réformes de la protection sociale: attentes, résultats actuels et devenir*, XXXème Rencontre de l'IPSE, Paris: IPSE.

Coleman, J. (1990) *Foundations of Social Theory*, Cambridge, MA: Harvard University Press.

Cormack, U. (1953) *The Welfare State (Royal Commission on the Poor Laws 1905-1909 and the Welfare State)*, Loch Memorial Lecture, London: Family Welfare Association.

Cox, R.H. (1998) 'The consequences of welfare state reform: how conceptions of social rights are changing', *Journal of Social Policy*, vol 27, no 1, pp 1-16.

Dawson, W. H. (1912) *Social Insurance in Germany*, London: T. Fisher Unwin.

Durand, P. (1953) 'Les équivoques de la redistribution du revenu par la sécurité sociale', *Droit social* (Paris).

EISS (European Institute for Social Security) (1986) *Sociological Research and Social Security – Proceedings of the European Institute for Social Security*, Deventer: Kluwer.

Esping-Andersen, G. (1990) *The Three Worlds of Welfare Capitalism*, Cambridge: Polity Press.

Ferge, Z. (2000) 'European integration and the reform of social security in the accession countries', Paper presented at a conference on economic and social dimensions of EU enlargement, Brussels, November.

Gill, I., Packard, T. and Yermo, J. (2005) *Keeping the Promise of Social Security in Latin America*, Washington, DC: Stanford University Press and World Bank.

Gillion, C. (2000) 'The development and reform of social security pensions: the approach of the International Labour Office', *International Social Security Review*, vol 53, no 1, pp 35-63.

Guinand, C. (2008) 'The creation of the ISSA and the ILO', *International Social Security Review*, vol 61, no 1, pp 81-98.

Higgins, J. (1981) *States of Welfare: Comparative Analysis in Social Policy*, Oxford: Blackwell.

ISSA (International Social Security Association) (1966) 'Round table meeting on the sociology of social security – Summary of proceedings', *Bulletin of the ISSA*, vol 19, nos 7-8, pp 235-241.

ISSA (1971) *The Planning of Social Security*, Studies and Research no 2, Geneva: ISSA.

ISSA (1973) *Current Issues in Social Security Planning: Concepts and Techniques*, Studies and Research no 4, Geneva: ISSA.

ISSA (1986) *The History of the International Social Security Association 1927–1987*, Geneva: ISSA.

ISSA (2009) *Survey on Social Security in Times of Crisis: Summary of Findings and Conclusions*, Geneva: ISSA.

Janne, H. (1967) 'Pour une sociologie de la sécurité sociale', in *Mélanges offerts à L.E. Troclet*, Brussels: Editions de l'Institut de Sociologie.

Kessler, F. (2005) 'A first inventory of new and revised approaches to social security', in ISSA *New and Revised Approaches to Social Protection in Europe*, European Series no 29, Geneva: ISSA.

Marshall, T. H. (1965) *Social Policy*, London: Hutchinson.

Mendelsohn, R. (1954) *Social Security in the British Commonwealth*, London: Athlone Press.

Mesa-Lago, C. (1978) *Social Security in Latin America: Pressure Groups, Stratification and Inequality*, Pittsburgh, PA: University of Pittsburgh Press.

Mesa-Lago, C. (1996) 'Pension system reforms in Latin America: the position of international organisations', *CEPAL Review*, no 60, pp 73-98.

Mesa-Lago, C. (2008) *Reassembling Social Security: A Survey of Pension and Health Care Reforms in Latin America*, Oxford: Oxford University Press.

Mesa-Lago, C. (2009) 'Re-reforms of Latin American pension systems: Argentinean and Chilean models and lessons', *The Geneva Papers on Risk and Insurance Issues and Practice*, Special Issue on the 'Four Pillars' Pensions, vol 34, no 4, pp 602-17.

Mièvre, J. (2005) 'Le solidarisme de Léon Bourgeois', *Cahiers de la Méditerranée*, vol 63, http://cdlm.revues.org/document17.html

MIRE-ISSA (1991) *Les comparaisons internationales des politiques et des systèmes de sécurité sociale*, Colloque de Recherche MIRE-ISSA, Paris: MIRE.

MIRE-ISSA (1992) *The International Comparisons of Social Security Policies and Systems*, MIRE-ISSA Research Symposium, Geneva: ISSA.

Moles, R. R. (1962) *Historia de Prevision Social en Hispanoamerica*, Buenos Aires: Ediciones Despalma.

Monnier, A. (1856) *Histoire de l'assistance dans les temps anciens et modernes*, Paris: Librairie de Guillaumin & Cie.

Müller, K. (2001) 'The political economy of pension reform in Eastern Europe', *International Social Security Review*, vol 54, nos 2-3, pp 57-79.

Mulligan, C. B., Gill, R. and Sala-i-Martin, X. (2002) *Social Security and Democracy*, NBER Working Paper no 8958, Cambridge, MA: NBER.

Munkova, G. (ed) (2004) *Socialni politika v evropskych zemich* [Social policy in European countries] (2nd edition), Prague: Karolinum.

Orenstein, M. A. (2000) *How Politics and Institutions affect Pension Reform in Three Post-Communist Countries*, Policy Research Working Paper. Washington, DC: World Bank.

Orszak, P. R. and Stiglitz, J. E. (1999) 'Rethinking pension reform: ten myths about social security systems', Paper presented to a conference on new ideas about old age security, World Bank, Washington, DC.

Oyen, E. (1986) 'The sociology of social security', Editorial introduction, *International Sociology*, vol 1, no 3, pp 219-21.

Palier, B. (2008) 'A long good bye to Bismarck? The politics of welfare reforms in continental Europe', *Italian Journal of Social Policy*, vol 1, pp 413-24.

Perrin, G. (1967) 'Pour une théorie sociologique de la sécurité sociale dans les sociétés industrielles', *Revue française de sociologie*, vol 8, no 3, pp 299-324.

Raphael, M. (1957) *The Origins of Public Superannuation Schemes in England, 1684-1859*, London: University of London.

Robson, W. A. (ed) (1948) *Social Security*, London: Allen and Unwin.

Room, G. (1979) *The Sociology of Welfare*, Oxford: Blackwell.

Rowntree, S. (1899) *Poverty: A Study of Town Life*, London: Macmillan.

Rys, V. (1964) 'The sociology of social security', *Bulletin of the ISSA*, vol 17, nos 1-2, pp 3-34.

Rys, V. (1966) 'Comparative studies of social security: problems and perspectives', *Bulletin of the ISSA*, nos 7-8, vol 19, pp 242-68.

Rys, V. (1999) *La sécurité sociale dans une société en transition: l'expérience tchèque*, Lausanne: Réalités Sociales.

Rys, V. (2002) 'Une décennie de réformes en Europe centrale: les facteurs qui déterminent l'évolution de la sécurité sociale', *Cahiers Genevois et Romands de Sécurité Sociale*, no 28, pp 9-19.

Scherman, K. G. (2005) 'The new Swedish pension system: more security or less?', in ISSA *New and Revised Approaches to Social Protection in Europe*, European Series no 29, Geneva: ISSA.

Sigg, R. (1986) 'The contribution of sociology to social security', *International Sociology*, vol 1, no 3, pp 283-95.

Taylor-Gooby, P. (2002) 'The silver age of the welfare state: perspectives on resilience', *International Social Policy*, vol 31, no 4, pp 597-622.

Townsend, P. (1975) *Sociology and Social Policy*, London: Allen Lane.

van Ginneken, W. and McKinnon R. (2007) 'Extending social security to all – introduction', *International Social Security Review*, vol 60, nos 2-3, pp 5-15.

Webb, S. and Webb, B. (1927) *English Local Government: The Old Poor Law*, London: Longman, Green.

World Bank (1994) *Averting the Old Age Crisis: Policies to Protect the Old and Promote Growth*, Washington, DC: Oxford University Press.

# Index

Page references for notes are followed by n